ASHE Higher Education Report: Vol.

Kelly Ward, Lisa E. Wolf-Wendel, Series Editors

Qualitative Inquiry for Equity in Higher Education: Methodological Innovations, Implications, and Interventions

Penny A. Pasque

Rozana Carducci

Aaron M. Kuntz

Ryan Evely Gildersleeve

Discover this journal online at

WILEY ONLINE LIBRARY

wileyonlinelibrary.com

Qualitative Inquiry for Equity in Higher Education: Methodological Innovations, Implications, and Interventions
Penny A. Pasque, Rozana Carducci, Aaron M. Kuntz, and Ryan Evely Gildersleeve
ASHE Higher Education Report: Volume 37, Number 6
Kelly Ward, Lisa E. Wolf-Wendel, Series Editors

Cover image by Birthe Lunau/©iStockphoto.

ISSN 1551-6970   electronic ISSN 1554-6306   ISBN 978-1-1183-7727-7

The ASHE Higher Education Report is part of the Jossey-Bass Higher and Adult Education Series and is published six times a year by Wiley Subscription Services, Inc., A Wiley Company, at Jossey-Bass, One Montgomery Street, Suite 1200, San Francisco, California 94104-4594.

For subscription information, see the Back Issue/Subscription Order Form in the back of this volume.

CALL FOR PROPOSALS: Prospective authors are strongly encouraged to contact Kelly Ward (kaward@wsu.edu) or Lisa Wolf-Wendel (lwolf@ku.edu). See "About the ASHE Higher Education Report Series" in the back of this volume.

Visit the Jossey-Bass Web site at **www.josseybass.com.**

Printed in the United States of America on acid-free recycled paper.

The ASHE Higher Education Report is indexed in CIJE: Current Index to Journals in Education (ERIC), Education Index/Abstracts (H.W. Wilson), ERIC Database (Education Resources Information Center), Higher Education Abstracts (Claremont Graduate University), IBR & IBZ: International Bibliographies of Periodical Literature (K.G. Saur), and Resources in Education (ERIC).

Advisory Board

The ASHE Higher Education Report Series is sponsored by the Association for the Study of Higher Education (ASHE), which provides an editorial advisory board of ASHE members.

Contents

Executive Summary

This monograph seeks to foster a dialogue on the future of qualitative inquiry for equity in higher education. Beginning with the premise that equity is of paramount concern in the study of higher education—permeating research on students, faculty, administration and governance, funding, educational policy, and so on—the text explores the promise and pitfalls of qualitative inquiry with respect to addressing issues of in/equity and fostering social change at micro, meso, and macro levels. Specifically, building upon five years of thought experiments and dialogic inquiry projects on the status of contemporary qualitative higher education scholarship, we advance a critique of the reductive and generic conceptions of qualitative research that dominate the field of higher education and call upon our higher education colleagues to examine the transformative potential embedded within critical qualitative inquiry.

The book's central argument is that equity-minded qualitative scholars of higher education can no longer simply fixate their critical eyes upon the *content* of their research (their object of analysis) but rather must extend their critical perspectives to the very methodological assumptions that make such content visible in particular ways. In more direct terms, we contend that investigations into manifestations of in/equity in higher education need to self-reflexively consider the ways in which research practices may actually serve to reinscribe the very in/equity the scholarship seeks to document and eradicate. This argument is consistent with the current eighth moment in qualitative research (Denzin and Lincoln, 2005b), which is concerned with critical conversations about democracy, race, gender, class, nation-states, globalization, freedom, and community. Importantly, the eighth moment is more than a focus on studying *about* these critical issues; the eighth moment strives to operationalize qualitative methodologies and congruent methods that directly reflect an emancipatory approach to research. In line with the eighth moment, we assert that critical qualitative inquiry, as an ever-expanding paradigm of understanding, provides a strategy by which to generate knowledge in service of equity and social justice.

Unfortunately, the epistemological and methodological perspectives associated with critical qualitative inquiry remain muted and marginalized within the higher education scholarly community, overshadowed by generic notions of qualitative research which offer little insight into the philosophical assumptions (matters of ontology, epistemology, axiology, methodology) that distinguish frameworks of inquiry such as post/positivism, constructivism, and critical inquiry. The absence of explicit discussions concerning researcher ways of knowing within the higher education scholarly community serves to reify dominant research paradigms that valorize the production of authoritative and deterministic truths, ultimately perpetuating the inequitable status quo.

Countering the limitations of dominant perspectives on qualitative inquiry in higher education, we highlight innovations and paradigmatic shifts particularly promising with respect to advancing higher education equity agendas. Consistent with the central argument of the book, these shifts occur at the level of philosophy, specifically ontology and epistemology, but have practical consequences with respect to how research can be thought of, designed, implemented, and shared. Unfortunately, discussions regarding innovative research practices fixate all-too-frequently on method, as though alterations to specialized techniques of research alone will bring about shifts in how we understand ourselves in relation to others, or draw new awareness to previously absent voices and identities within higher education scholarship. We hope to change such thinking—to challenge readers to resist simplistic notions of innovative methods in favor of more epistemological and ontological concerns, and to do so in the name of equity and inquiry for social justice in higher education. We anchor our argument in specific examples, elaborating on the innovations arising from work on dialogic inquiry, embodied knowledge, and critical geography—all three approaches to inquiry with implications at the level of epistemology and methodology and which contribute to revolutionary research capable of affecting material social change within institutions and systems of higher education.

Cognizant of the fact that higher education scholars are currently working in era of methodological conservatism (Denzin and Giardina, 2006; Lincoln and Cannella, 2004a, 2004b) defined by organizational practices and principles of inquiry that actively undermine the adoption of critical epistemological and methodological perspectives, we present a candid discussion of the tensions and challenges encountered by higher education scholars seeking to engage in methodologically innovative scholarship. Specifically, the text examines the increasing dominance of two inextricably connected disciplining discourse regimes—academic capitalism and scientifically based educational research—and takes up the question, "What is at stake for both historically marginalized communities and critical qualitative higher education scholars if dominant post/positivist methodological perspectives continue to frame the principles and practices of higher education inquiry?"

The implications of methodological conservatism for individuals and communities who regularly encounter individual, institutional, and/or societal oppression include the preservation of discriminatory educational practices, policies, and environments and perpetuation of the inequitable status quo. Higher education scholars who dare to disrupt, interrogate, and challenge the disciplining regimes of truth that characterize methodologically conservative promotion and tenure standards, funding and publication peer review processes, as well as human subjects research approval are subject to professional censure and scholarly punishments (for example, diminished funding and publication opportunities) that undercut the norms of academic freedom and job security historically associated with tenure track and tenured faculty positions. Our aim in shedding light on the material consequences associated with methodological innovation is not to discourage critical higher education scholars from engaging in transformative scholarship, but rather to raise awareness of the consequences that may stem from enacting critical methodological commitments in the hopes of better preparing critical scholars to productively navigate and overcome professional roadblocks.

In the monograph's final chapter, we issue a call to action through intervention, drawing upon extant qualitative methodology scholarship to describe numerous opportunities and strategies for confronting the oppressive knowledge systems that undermine the equity aims of critical qualitative higher education research. Specifically, we highlight the transformative potential embedded in researcher reflexivity activities, participation in institutional and organizational activism (for example, membership on institutional review boards, promotion and tenure committees, conference planning teams, etc.), new approaches to socializing emerging scholars to the roles and responsibilities of academe, and the cultivation of the abilities associated with speaking to and collaborating with multiple constituencies within and beyond the academy.

Without a doubt, actively engaging in efforts to expand one's understandings of emancipatory epistemologies, becoming social media savvy, transforming educational inquiry curricula, and initiating change from within organizations as members of influential committees while simultaneously meeting traditional promotion and tenure expectations is emotionally and physically exhausting work. We believe, however, it is far more costly to perpetuate dominant traditions of qualitative inquiry that fail to address the fundamental philosophical underpinnings of in/equity in higher education. We contend that critical qualitative inquiry toward educational equity need not always be about immediate large revolution in terms of the grand sense of things, but may happen through daily practices of intervention. Small steps that build toward radical transformation cannot be underestimated. We invite both emerging and seasoned critical higher education scholars to interrupt the violence of methodological conservatism and answer the call to action through intentional contributions to cumulative social change and educational equity.

Foreword

Calls for research that are relevant and geared toward change abound on many college campuses. Educational researchers are often at the forefront of leading conversations about some of the critical topics related to research methods and methodologies. Penny Pasque, Rozana Carducci, Aaron Kuntz, and Ryan Gildersleeve in this monograph grapple with some of the critical issues facing researchers wanting to make a difference with their research. Emerging scholars, in particular, often find themselves constrained by calls for "objectivity" and "distance" in their research. Dominant discourses related to research that are often taught in graduate school direct students toward perspectives that are disconnected from passion and place. Researchers can find themselves in a quandary: do I meet the conventions of traditional research perspectives or can I make meaningful and critical contributions to the vexing problems facing education today? This monograph gives permission and validity to research approaches that incorporate critical perspectives, but more importantly, it offers readers the tools necessary to carry out research that is geared toward social justice, equity, and change.

The authors call for research that is intentional in its approach to create social change geared toward the ends of justice and equity. This monograph does an excellent job of identifying some of the key issues associated with engaging in critical qualitative research and also provides readers with the tools necessary to carry out research that is aligned with social change. This monograph helps bring to light the need to "generate knowledge for equity and justice." Many of the problems facing higher education today call for bold approaches to understanding that move beyond mere description. A critical approach to qualitative research inherently ties theory and practice, with an eye toward theoretical approaches that unveil the often oppressive practices that maintain the status quo. Too often researchers, even well-meaning ones, are descriptive and passive bystanders in the educational arena. The authors in this monograph compel researchers to get off the sidelines to contribute to action and to use research to bring about change. Although not about "action research" per se, the monograph instead is a call to critical action—action that generates knowledge that is direct in showing problems of inequity.

Colleges of Education, especially in light of budget cuts, are in a unique situation to provide leadership related to the problems facing all levels of education. Many of these problems are associated with inequities in schools, communities, and college campuses. As a community of scholars, educational researchers are well suited to take a lead in addressing the inequities that exist, but to do so calls for knowledge generation and research that is grounded in perspectives that reveal and call for change. Doctoral programs have been taking the lead in some of these conversations, given the knowledge generated in dissertation research. In recent years many graduate programs in education have grappled with redesigning their doctoral experiences around issues of transformation, social justice, equity, and change. It's easy to identify convictions associated with social change tied to education, but carrying out research that aligns with such goals is often elusive. This monograph provides theoretical and practical information about moving from the ideal of research for equity and change to the reality of research that contributes to agendas that promote social justice.

Qualitative Inquiry for Equity in Higher Education is sure to be of use to emerging scholars who are compelled toward questions and convictions geared toward change, but lack the understanding and the background to carry out such research. Seasoned scholars looking to move their research from description to the next level of action will also find the monograph useful. Practitioners wanting to shed new light on problems of practice will find the monograph helpful to identify issues and provide insight into methodologies that reveal underlying problems and their solutions. Scholars interested in issues associated with methodology will find this monograph particularly useful given its conviction and also the information the authors provide related to theory and practice. The monograph is a must-read for students, faculty, and staff tired of business as usual and wanting to use fresh approaches to their research and to bring about change in educational settings related to equity.

Kelly Ward and Lisa Wolf-Wendel
Series Editors

Acknowledgments

The authors would like to thank Jason Evans, Graduate Research Assistant in Educational Leadership and Policy Analysis at the University of Missouri, for his support in the preparation of this manuscript.

Published online in Wiley Online Library
(wileyonlinelibrary.com) • DOI: 10.1002/aehe.3706

Qualitative Inquiry for Equity in Higher Education

THE STUDY OF HIGHER EDUCATION MUST confront ever-changing cartographies of power and politics that extend from the postmodern condition. Contemporary calls for increased accountability point to the complexity of human experience and, often, refuse a consensus on the measure(s) to which institutions should be held accountable (Burke, 2005; Dee, 2006; Tierney, 2006). Further, funding and revenue generation precariously rest in the politics of an increasingly economically disenfranchised public and their legislative representatives, while private enterprise shows an increasing interest in strengthening its influence on and within higher education. All the while, multiple conservative forces (neoliberalism, neoconservatism, authoritarian populist religious conservatives) collude to gain control over various dimensions of the academic endeavor (Apple, 2006a, 2006b). For example, the standards movement from K–12 education pops into the public imagery as a potentially viable solution for maintenance of their investment in public higher education. As these efforts, campaigns, collusions, exercises, and investments contribute to shifting—and shape shifting—systems and institutions of tertiary education around the globe (Cheek, 2007; Curtis, 2008; Morgan, 2004; St. Pierre, 2004; Torrance, 2008, 2011), American higher education scholars beg questions of fairness, opportunity, egalitarianism, merit, equality, and basic ontological interest in postsecondary education.

Importantly, the assumptions that govern inquiry into such questions are not immune from such power-laden discourses. That is to say, scholars of higher education cannot simply fixate their critical eyes upon the *content* of their research (their object of analysis) but must extend such criticality to the very methodological assumptions that make such content visible in particular ways. Thus, investigations into particular manifestations of in/equity in higher education need to self-reflexively consider the ways in which research practices may actually serve to reinscribe the very in/equity the scholarship seeks to document and eradicate. As a consequence, we begin this monograph with a passionate investment in the critical interrogation of research practices and their inherent link to our understanding of the world in which we live. More specifically, we take as the subject of this text the intersection of qualitative approaches to inquiry and questions of in/equity in higher education as a field of study. Given the considerable stakes (for students, faculty, administrators, and the general public) regarding in/equity in higher education, ours is an unapologetic advocacy for critical qualitative approaches to inquiry—an inquiry practice that engages with and intervenes within the dominant discourses of our times.

Throughout this text, we situate inquiry as political activity and, as such, refuse suggestions that research practices are in some way immune to the normalizing discourses of our times. Further, we point to the multiple ways in which traditional methodological approaches have (re)produced the very inequities and injustices that plague our contemporary context. Given the present circumstances of our world, there remains little time or space for conciliatory orientations toward social change. We thus offer our readers an invitation to critical dialogue concerning the implications of inquiry practices on questions of in/equity in tertiary education. We seek an audience that refuses the inadequate stance of disinterestedness in favor of critical engagement—the willingness to work for change even as we ourselves are changed by such work.

As is detailed later in this chapter, *equity,* as a concept, provides a unifying political goal for scholars interested in fostering social justice in, by, through, and for the social institution of higher education. Equity involves considerations of an ongoing array of social processes and institutions and their subsequent impact on select social groups; the ways in which such social arrangements disadvantage some groups and legitimate others. Considerations for equity call forth issues of justness and fairness as well as strategies aimed at accounting for historical lineages of inequality. Unfortunately, issues of equity rarely make their way into methodological discussions or, if they are addressed, such discussions inevitably remain at the level of method—those techniques aimed at accounting for or documenting the production of inequitable circumstance. As a response to this absence in higher education scholarship on equity, we offer critical qualitative inquiry.

Norman Denzin (2010b) describes critical inquiry as "a form of activism, of critique" (p. 34). In this way, "critical scholars are committed to showing how the practices of critical, interpretive qualitative research can help change the world in positive ways" (p. 25). This perspective is characteristic of the eighth moment in qualitative research (Denzin and Lincoln, 2005b),[1] which is concerned with critical conversations about democracy, race, gender, class, nation-states, globalization, freedom, and community. Importantly, the contemporary moment is more than a focus on studying *about* these critical issues; the eighth moment strives to operationalize qualitative methodologies and congruent methods that directly reflect an emancipatory approach to research. In line with the eighth moment, we find that critical qualitative inquiry, as an ever-expanding paradigm of understanding, provides a strategy by which to generate knowledge in service of equity and social justice. Unfortunately, the epistemological and methodological perspectives associated with critical qualitative inquiry remain muted and marginalized within the higher education scholarly community. Hence, the need for this monograph.

This monograph is meant for qualitative scholars of higher education who share concerns regarding in/equity in higher and postsecondary education. It is also meant for an audience who wants inquiry to do more than simply describe the status quo; such readers seek critical interventions into institutional inequity through the research process. We see these as the goals for critical qualitative inquiry. As Denzin and Giardina (2010) note, "It is not *just* about 'method' or 'technique.' Rather, *qualitative research is about making the world visible in ways that implement the goals of social justice and radical, progressive democracy*" (p. 14; original emphasis). We seek to make the world newly visible in the name of social justice—critical qualitative inquiry as a radical democratic act. As a consequence, we hope to provide a broad framework for understanding how qualitative inquiry may be useful in understanding the inequitable world-as-it-is and helpful in imagining a more equitable world-as-it-could-be. To be clear, we argue that dominant traditions of qualitative inquiry fail to address the fundamental philosophical underpinnings of in/equity in higher education. Therefore, we put forth that critical and post-modern paradigms become essential for equity scholarship in higher education. Indeed, we will spend most of our pages discussing paradigmatic shifts, methodological innovations, and attendant issues involved in what we broadly name as "critical qualitative inquiry for equity in higher education."

In thinking of this monograph and why yet another text about qualitative research was warranted, we came to three orienting questions. The first two address basic desires: "Why consider qualitative research in higher education?" and "Has qualitative inquiry met its promises?" We came to these questions after mulling through thought experiments and dialogic inquiry projects on the status and limitations of contemporary qualitative higher education scholarship (see Carducci and others, 2007; Gildersleeve and Kuntz, 2011; Pasque, Carducci, Gildersleeve, and Kuntz, 2011; Pasque, Kuntz, Carducci, and Gildersleeve, 2008). During our preparatory inquiry, we pondered if qualitative research has met its promises in higher education. Are the historic promises made by the narrative (Chase, 2005; Daiute and Lightfoot, 2004), case study (Merriam, 2009; Stake, 1995, 2008; Yin, 2003, 2009), ethnographic (Atkinson and others, 2001; Hammersley and Atkinson, 2007; Van Maanen, 2011), phenomenology (Moustakas, 1994; Pollio, Henley, and Thompson, 1997; van Manen, 1990), and grounded theory (Corbin and Strauss, 2008; Glaser and Strauss, 1967) vogues in higher education as productive as once thought? Can the liberatory imperative of qualitative inquiry be realized in higher education studies? These questions speak to philosophical and material needs of the people that populate, benefit from, and contribute to—as well as those who remain marginalized by—American higher education. As such, the qualitative study of such a social institution demands methodological attention.

As critical scholars, we collectively privilege the relationship of knowledge to sociopolitical–historical contexts in our own work. As such, we follow up our basic desire with a third question of significance. We ask, "What is at stake for critical qualitative inquiry as higher education faces dramatic social shifts in the twenty-first century?" Again we drew upon our thought experiments and dialogic inquiry. We were moved by investigations of how increasingly globalized and capitalized human resources might shift or augment the responsibilities of higher education researchers. We are interested in the unique and necessary role(s) that critical qualitative inquiry might play in the changing responsibilities and emphases of American higher education. And again, we assume these concerns must be pursued within an ethical imperative for equity and democratic opportunity.

In many ways, this text seeks to problematize research practices into in/equity in higher education. In line with the approach of Michel Foucault (1987), Marshall (2007) notes that the notion of problematization involves "a freedom to detach oneself from what one does . . . so as to establish it as an *object of thought* and to reflect upon it as a problem" (p. 20). Importantly, this freedom to step back remains a significant first step of the critical process. The critical pause allows the inquirer to make strange the familiar, to ask questions of commonsensical strategies and practices that might otherwise escape notice. As Foucault (1987) asserts, critical thought begins with problematization, the necessity "for a certain number of factors" to make the known "uncertain, to have made it lose its familiarity, or to have provoked a certain number of difficulties around it" (p. 117). This monograph both encourages and enacts critical pause, seeking to problematize qualitative inquiry into and for equity in higher education.

As an effort at problematization, it is important to note from the beginning what this text does not do. We do not provide a detailed review of specific qualitative data collection and analysis methods or techniques that follow each methodology or research strategy. Such reviews have been aptly captured by multiple previous research methods texts (Bogdan and Biklen, 2006; Cameron, 2001; Charmaz, 2005; Clarke, 2005, 2007; Corbin and Strauss, 2008; Daiute and Lightfoot, 2004; Denzin, 2003; Emerson, Fretz, and Shaw, 1995; Esterberg, 2002; Fontana and Prokos, 2007; Hart, 1998; Hesse-Biber, 2007a, 2007b; Johnstone, 2002; Marshall and Rossman, 2011; Merriam, 2002; Miles and Huberman, 1994; Morse and others, 2009; Norris, 2009; Rossman and Rallis, 2011; Spry, 2011; van Manen, 1990, 2002, 2007; Warren and Karner, 2010; Weiss, 1994; Wetherell, Taylor, and Yates, 2001; Wilson, 2009; Yin, 2009). Furthermore, such a mechanistic review would be counterproductive to the broader conversation we hope to ignite through our arguments about the consequences for scholars' ways of knowing within inquiry efforts that purportedly promote equity in higher education. In short, we are not interested in approaching these issues through the specter of technique, but rather the logic formations and regimes of power that make select approaches and orientations visible (or absent).

We also do not engage in this text with what some term "critical quantitative research." Notably, critical quantitative work is absent from this project because we have yet to encounter an engaged articulation of such scholarship that ably presents an approach in line with our notions of *critical* outlined above. For example, in her introduction to *New Directions for Institutional Research,* No. 133, devoted to "using quantitative data to answer critical questions," Stage (2007) advocates for a critical quantitative approach as a means to question, modify, or create new models that describe those who are the objects of educational research. Again, our work as critical qualitative researchers is to move beyond the descriptive and toward active intervention in systematized processes of social injustice. As such, we do not see our work as in opposition to the position articulated by Stage (or others who espouse her approach), but differently aligned and intentioned. In addition, our aim here is not to engage in the over-trodden and no longer productive paths of "paradigm wars" that have plagued the academy (Denzin, 2010b). Our expertise is in qualitative inquiry and, as a consequence, our practices extend from this particular paradigmatic positioning.

In sum, we are in favor of critical approaches congruent with the eighth moment of qualitative inquiry (Denzin and Lincoln 2005b) that resist methodological conservatism (Denzin and Giardina, 2006; Lincoln and Cannella, 2004a, 2004b), seek to self-reflexively intervene in normalizing discourses, and work for social justice through inquiry to improve the human condition. To that end, we focus our attention in this text on the epistemological and methodological implications of conducting critical qualitative inquiry for equity in higher education.

On Equity

This monograph is predicated on the assertion that equity is a paramount concern in the study of higher education. As such, we take equity as our central organizing analytic—that to which all other arguments must contribute and work to achieve. We find equity especially fitting for this role, as it permeates any and all facets of the study of higher education. Equity concerns can be found in the organization of higher education institutions and their governance, funding, campus life, relationship to broader society, and proximal communities. Equity concerns litter the landscape of academic work: faculty livelihoods, labor practices, academic freedom, tenure, and the curriculum. Equity concerns plague the (re)generation of knowledge: funding agencies, productivity expectations, prestige indexes, and the truncation of knowledge through capitalist practices. Equity concerns are foundational to students' lives: marginalized identities, opportunity to learn, access, persistence, attainment, pedagogy, and the social stratification produced by participation in higher education. Clearly, *equity* can be useful to explore higher education from micro, mezzo, macro, and transgressive levels of analysis.

Equity also resists definition. As criticalists, we resist defining it in narrow, deterministic, and unitary terms. We favor a more fluid, dynamic, and pluralistic understanding of what equity may mean in opposition to a fixed notion of what equity must or should explain. In this way, our understanding of equity extends from discussions regarding "what is equity" or "what is equitable" even as it inherently draws upon concerns regarding the means by which the practices of tertiary education might intervene within and/or reproduce normative/normalizing social discourses.

Furthermore, we see equity as inextricably linked to social justice and social change. Indeed, these three concepts are seen as interdependent from our critical perspectives. Operationally, equity is that which affords us the ability to make power relations visible—demonstrating where and when in social experiences power produces differential experiences within our social institutions (Bloom, 2009; Denzin and Giardina, 2009; hooks, 1998; Kincheloe, 2005). Social justice serves as our compulsion to document not only how these power relations produce oppressive and/or emancipatory conditions but also how to imagine rearranging these relations to map new conditions that achieve an ever expansive notion of equity and opportunity. In these ways, social justice requires a commitment to connect the individual to the institutional to the social. Social justice demands a systemic point of view and commitment to systemic change. Social change is that which emerges from the critical commitment of praxis—moving the imagined into reality albeit in dynamic, pluralistic, idiosyncratic, and contextually contingent manifestations. But, alas, we contend it is less useful to trifurcate these concepts apart from one another, and thus, throughout this monograph we take very little pains to clarify when we speak of equity, social justice, or social change. Rather, we assume that using one implies the rest.

Contemporary Contexts of Higher Education Research

Equity's centrality in the study of higher education, and the roles of critical qualitative inquiry in addressing such concerns, must be understood against American higher education's contemporary contexts. In turn, American higher education today must be understood in relation to sociopolitical (including economic), cultural, and historical contexts. Today's problems are produced from complex interactions and intersections of social and political forces that have emerged and evolved over time.

Sociopolitical Contexts

American higher education in the early twenty-first century struggles to define itself against a backdrop of globalization and within sociopolitical markers of academic capitalism (Slaughter and Rhoades, 2004), conservative modernization (Apple, 2006a, 2006b), and methodological conservatism (Denzin and Giardina, 2006; Lincoln and Cannella, 2004a, 2004b). The nexus of these contextual dimensions begs attention and commands nuanced understandings of how equity, critical qualitative inquiry, and the study of higher education may be pursued.

The *globalization* of economic resources, capital, culture, knowledge generation, and sharing has become ubiquitous. Conceptually, globalization has been ascribed multiple and at times conflicting definitions, but a basic understanding holds a common assumption that resources, capital, culture, and knowledge are now—and seemingly will forever be—interrelated across national, regional, and even hemispheric boundaries (Burbules and Torres, 2000). Clear examples of globalization's significance in the contemporary context of American higher education can be seen in the global economic crisis (Krugman, 2009; Zemsky, 2005), wherein people and governments across the planet find themselves victims of the very economic tools and instruments that were once thought to promote indestructible wealth. Yet, simultaneously, the global community has seen the rise of nascent states that challenge and/or trouble dominant economic practices. For example, Brazil's economy, although tenuous, has boomed in its resistance to borrowing from transnational economic agencies like the International Monetary Fund and the World Bank (Brown, 2009; DeCarvalho, 2002). China has strategically and selectively invited capitalist companies into its borders and seen unprecedented economic growth in times of global economic recession (Bijian, 2005; Mahbubani, 2005).

The influence of globalization on American higher education has yet to be sufficiently theorized, much less exhaustively documented (for discussion of globalization and higher education in the Americas, see Rhoads and Torres, 2005). And, indeed, such documentation may not be a worthwhile project, as circumstances will certainly shift and change much more quickly than can be accounted. Yet, deeper theories of the interplay between globalizing practices, processes, and principles with American higher education must be developed. Such theories could help explain the significance and influence of individual institutions' international efforts (for example, American campuses within foreign borders), as well as a myriad of other globally involved efforts (for example, international research teams) directly and indirectly implicated by American higher education.

Related to the globalization of higher education, *academic capitalism* has been theorized, documented, and discussed at length (Bok, 2003; Giroux and Giroux, 2004; Ikenberry, 2009; Slaughter and Leslie, 1997; Slaughter and Rhoades, 2004). In essence, academic capitalism signifies the presence of capitalist values and practices in academe. Principal among these highlighted in the literature are the big money practices and dependence of research universities on funded research. Other features of academic capitalism include the increased influence of market forces within and across academe. For example, student services, such as housing, have become increasingly privatized. College admissions are implicated in an ever-increasing influence of market forces such as private college counseling and college rankings like those found in *U.S. News and World Report* (McDonough, 1997; McDonough, Antonio, and Walpole, 1998).

A broader understanding of the contemporary sociopolitical contexts of American higher education can be described by incorporating what Michael Apple (2006a, 2006b) termed the *conservative modernization* of education. In brief, conservative modernization notates the intersections of neoliberalism, neoconservatism, populist fundamentalism, and managerialism as a hegemonic bloc whose interests converge to dominate knowledge generation and education broadly. Marked by neoliberal notions of accountability, neoconservative ideas of what counts as knowledge, populist fundamentalist notions of history, and managerialist interests in the status quo, this hegemonic bloc weaves powerful narratives about (higher) education and its reflection or production of social values. We have written elsewhere about the increasing conservative modernization of academia (Gildersleeve, Kuntz, Pasque, and Carducci, 2010), noting ways that the hegemonic bloc has informed how scholars, policy makers, and popular audiences think about the social relationship between American higher education and the public.

Directly in opposition to the onset of critical qualitative efforts to describe, understand, and explain the above social contexts, American higher education today, writ large, is mired in *methodological conservatism* (Denzin and Giardina, 2006; Lincoln and Cannella, 2004a, 2004b). Fueled by an environment obsessed with objective knowledge, replicable and/or experimental inquiry, and narrow definitions of reliable "data," methodological conservatism indicates not only strong social, governmental, and institutional preferences for positivistic science but the actual truncation of knowledge, particularly knowledge generated by critical, postmodern, and other dissident methodological traditions. This scientistic fetishism (Lather, 2006, 2007) informs a new politics of evidence (Denzin and Giardina, 2009), demonstrating the marginalization of nondominant paradigms in social research. This methodological conservatism presents particular dangers to critical inquiry generally, and critical qualitative approaches to in/equity in higher education more specifically. As noted earlier, these discourses collude to present a challenging and complex contemporary context, particularly concerning manifestations of in/equity in higher education. We believe inquiry has a responsibility to interrogate such circumstances, and to do so with an open and communicated agenda of advocacy and social justice.

On Dangers

Famously, Michel Foucault (1983) opined that "everything is dangerous, which is not exactly the same as bad. If everything is dangerous then we always have something to do. So my position leads not to apathy but to hyper—and pessimistic—activism" (p. 232). We share this position of hyperpessimistic activism and remain attuned to the dangers inherent in inquiry approaches to higher education. As Denzin and Giardina (2010) note, such activism links both pointing to and challenging injustice: "critical qualitative inquiry scholars are united in the commitment to expose and critique the forms of inequality and discrimination that operate in daily life" (p. 16).

As will be discussed in later chapters, we contend that the most dominant methodologies used in qualitative higher education research operate from post/positivist assumptions about the social world. As such, we are wary of their potential to address equity concerns in any sort of fundamental or systemic fashion. Rather, we believe that post/positivist assumptions reinscribe the very same ideologies that make inequity so rampantly plausible in society. Chief among these are the naturalized beliefs that an unequivocable "truth" does exist and therefore, an individual unified subject (that is, identity) can be known (Brown and Strega, 2005; Clough, 2007; Crotty, 1998). These naturalized assumptions of the world create a hegemonic circumference of a knowledge base where truth and identity are seen as neutral objects in the social world—even those researchers who argue for constructed meanings (as in constructionist epistemes) fall trap to the neutrality of their analytic objects. To borrow from our earlier language, such discourses privilege intense discussions of technique and inquiry procedures while ignoring critical concerns regarding the systems of logic that inform them. Effectively, exercises and relations of power are left null, void, or completely absent from analysis (Brown and Strega, 2005; Noblit, Flores, and Murillo, 2004). The abstraction of such analyses all too often becomes normalized through incongruous or intentionally masked philosophies of knowledge perpetrated by such post/positivistic thinking. As such, hidden agendas permeate the landscape of the dominant methodologies, which in turn undermine radically democratic social change for equity and social justice.

As feminist scholars have explored, a unified subject disingenuously inscribes identities as fixed and stable onto bodies (Bloom, 1998; Talburt, 2000). Conceptualizing stable identities allows for a politic of identity to form, which dangerously sets expectations of conformity, inherently relies upon us-versus-them logics of conflict, and becomes easily quantified into notions of human capital, where some capital will become more valuable than others in crass calculations of human experience. As such, qualitative research that relies upon, reinscribes, or produces unified subjects can be dangerous to the pursuits of equity and social justice.

Fundamentally, these dangers manifest from obscured notions of power, agency, and resistance. As criticalists, we recognize multiple notions of these concepts, and as a collective, we deploy them differently across our own research agendas. However, we stand in consensus that all inquiry, particularly in the field of higher education, *must theorize explicitly* power, agency, and resistance, in order to interrogate the inequitable social relations that plague society. Explicit and deep understandings of these key concepts in qualitative inquiry are necessary if scholars want to understand how American higher education produces, reflects, and gets ensnared by inequality and injustice. Agency and resistance, in particular, are paramount in the desire for higher education to address concerns of equity and justice.

Responding to Dangers

We find traditional methodological assumptions to misstep/reinscribe inequality and therefore we focus our "call to arms" in a critical paradigm that accounts for the postmodern condition (as context/epoch/"new" realities) and articulates power relations in the world as it is (understood) while working toward reimagining the world as it could be. As such, we name our critical qualitative inquiry as decidedly politically engaged research. The choices made to seek understanding and explanation of the social world, be they philosophical (such as methodological) or technical (such as methods), carry political consequence. In order to counter the hidden agendas of inquiry briefly introduced earlier, politically engaged critical qualitative inquiry seeks to make the politic of our research congruent with the methodological decisions deployed throughout our inquiry.

Further, we see critical qualitative work as a response to—and intervention within—traditional research paradigms, and therefore, we challenge long-held beliefs and guiding assumptions of what social research in higher education can and/or must entail. For example, we find inspiration in Susan Talburt's (2004) questioning of the importance of data verification strategies, such as member checking. We appreciate the difficult workings of wondering why respondents might be more or less the authority of their experience at different moments in the inquiry. And we value troubling the authority of human experience.

Finally, as advocates of a critical qualitative inquiry for equity in higher education, we accept, appreciate, and promote the notion that research can and should provide alternative and pluralistic ways of coming to know the social world. We need multiple, competing, and conflicting renderings of reality so as to offer up tensions where more deliberate and informed choices can be made. We argue that values-laden research cannot be escaped, but rather should be exposed so as to become engendered with historical values that can effect social change. These are methodological principles we find marked by silence in much of the prevailing higher education literature. As such, and by way of this monograph, we initiate a critical conversation that takes seriously the political and ideological nature of dialogue, a key element of critical inquiry explored in the next chapter. We seek to interrupt this silence by initiating dialogue among higher education scholars on the principles and tools of methodological conservatism as well as the implications of these "dangerous discourses" (Lincoln and Cannella, 2004a) for scholars committed to addressing issues of in/equity in postsecondary educational institutions.

Outline of the Monograph

In order to scaffold our arguments as a pedagogical conversation, we begin in "Confronting Qualitative Inquiry in Higher Education" by discussing qualitative methodology from its philosophical foundations into its contemporary instantiations. We base this discussion in the dynamic intersection of ontological, epistemological, and axiological assumptions—what we term the *interactive triad* that is essential to the critical examination of inquiry. Briefly, we offer an overview of how post/positivistic approaches to inquiry have failed (even undermined) equity aims in higher education. Countering these limitations of the dominant paradigms in qualitative research methodology in higher education, we highlight innovations and paradigmatic shifts that we find promising for higher education scholars to consider. These shifts occur at the level of philosophy, but have practical consequences to how research can be thought of, designed, implemented, and shared. We juxtapose traditional approaches with a thorough presentation of how critical inquiry counters post/positivistic claims even as it makes possible space for intervention in dominant discourses surrounding in/equity in higher education.

"Critical Concerns for Qualitative Inquiry in Higher Education" situates these discussions historically, beginning with the recognition that 2012 is the ten-year anniversary of the National Research Council's (NRC, 2002) *Scientific Research in Education*, a catalyst for much discussion regarding the aims, scope, and normalization of inquiry in the field of education. Throughout the chapter, we acknowledge the challenges and tensions encountered by critical qualitative higher education scholars seeking to engage in methodologically innovative scholarship within the contemporary era of methodological conservatism. Specifically, we examine the disciplining discourses of scientifically based educational research and academic capitalism and explore what is at stake for both higher education scholars and the historically marginalized communities they seek to work with if research on educational inequity continues to be framed by these conservative regimes of truth (Foucault, 1980).

Finally, in "Opportunities for Resisting Methodological Conservatism" we share a call to action in order to push beyond critique for critique sake, highlighting individual as well as organizational opportunities for intervention aimed at cultivating research that advances social change and educational equity. However, as much as we strive for the production of utopian texts to help us understand the social institution of higher education, we are not unaware of the attendant issues of concern produced by them. Rather, we present vigilantly engaged and reflexive analyses of potential threats, dangers, and unrelenting concerns associated with the paradigmatic shift–shaping that we call for throughout the monograph. Specifically, we engage with concerns related to the commodification and truncation of knowledge and the continued stranglehold of methodological conservatism in academe.

Challenge to the Reader

In concluding our introductory arguments, we would like to issue a challenge to you, the readers. We ask that as you consider the arguments we scaffold throughout the monograph, you also try to imagine a future of higher education research as driven by inquiry developed out of critical frameworks that recognize contemporary contexts of higher and postsecondary education. In this way, this monograph serves as the impetus for a dialogue between authors and readers about the future of qualitative inquiry for equity in higher education. Ours is an open text, purposively resistive to the tight and full closure that marks objective and known truths. As such, we hope that what follows provokes response, challenges practices, and encourages interventions in the name of social justice and equity in higher education.

Confronting Qualitative Inquiry in Higher Education

A S AN APPLIED AND INTERDISCIPLINARY field of study, higher education has incredible opportunity to draw on a wealth of scholarly traditions in order to critique the status quo, interrogate power, theorize agency, and work toward social justice. The study of higher education is not bound by any one discipline or its methods. Rather, scientists, humanists, artists, therapists, architects, critics, activists, and many more could potentially populate the scholarly landscape. As an applied field, the study of higher education could draw from any and all scholarly traditions where new methodologies and methods could be forged. Cultural studies of race, gender, and sexuality could be brought into concert and contest with design aesthetics and principles from engineering or quantum physics. Artists could draw on the technologies of Geographic Information Systems and help render new understandings of how funding practices disenfranchise collaborative work, even as funding sources increasingly call for multisited and mixed-methods projects. With all of this potential for cross-, inter-, and/or transdisciplinary scholarship, equity could be championed and inequality could be slayed. The study of higher education could potentially harness tools to tackle the most nuanced problems of inequality in one of society's most integral institutions.

It does not.

Rather, the study of higher education repeats. Social science methods, predicated on positivist assumptions, dominate the scholarly landscape in the study of higher education—even in the qualitative study of higher education. Most published research findings are predictable and even when studies share something new, it rarely surprises. The wheel keeps turning. The canon of today looks surprisingly similar to the canon of yesterday. Innovations today will ring somewhat vaguely familiar to innovations tomorrow. Certainly, new lines of inquiry within higher education have developed. A field that began largely with sociological and economic analyses has added some cultural, political, and psychological analyses. A field that once focused on the study of organizations now pays attention to the individuals that populate those organizations. On occasion, broader strokes are drawn in the storytelling of higher education research, and notably, what once was a field that seemed obsessed with the wealthy white male perspective and experience has made dramatic efforts to include women, people of color, and people from less affluent privileges. The field has grown, undeniably. But we ask, has the field changed, ontologically?

Undoubtedly, higher education in America was established as an exclusionary institution. Its history is rife with examples of how certain persons were made to benefit from higher education, while others were not. As a social institution, higher education has been held up as a promise of opportunity, an engine of growth, and a vehicle for change in American society. Yet, among the predictable analyses found from the now well-established canons of higher education scholarship, we can state with confidence that inequality exists and, indeed, is perpetuated through the social institution of higher education. We argue that while the study of higher education has grown, much of this growth has been from a reductionist, additive model. This may sound counterintuitive, but our point is that simply adding more of the philosophically hegemonic disciplines to the practice of the study of higher education does little to effect social change through such inquiry. Including more voices definitely diversifies the perspectives within post/positivistic thought, and clearly assists the field in paying more attention to how more and different people experience the institution. But this additive model has done little to effect real change in the very real inequities that plague higher education and local communities.

The aims of this chapter are threefold. In the first section, we elaborate on our critique of qualitative research in higher education, highlighting the ways in which dominant paradigms of inquiry reify generic approaches to qualitative research ill-equipped to substantively address issues of educational in/equity. We then challenge higher education scholars to move beyond discussions of qualitative method and technique in the interest of exploring the implications for equity embedded within a researcher's ontological, epistemological, axiological, and methodological assumptions and principles. Building on our call for more explicit and deep engagement in the philosophy of higher education inquiry, we introduce the epistemological and methodological underpinnings of critical qualitative inquiry and elaborate on our argument that realizing the transformative potential of higher education research necessitates movement toward innovative epistemological and methodological perspectives. We anchor this argument in specific examples, highlighting multiple innovative approaches to issues of voice, the construction of the research subject, and representation in critical qualitative inquiry.

Brief Notes on Qualitative Research in Higher Education Scholarship

Before examining the promise of critical qualitative inquiry in our field, it remains important to explicate the contemporary context of research in higher education. As noted, post/positivist paradigms dominate social science. Despite claims by scholars such as Egon Guba and Yvonna Lincoln (2005) suggesting that postmodernism, critical theory, and constructivism have gained legitimacy and are well established in a manner that is at least equal to conventional paradigms, we do not consider this to be the case in the field of higher education. Indeed, the 2010–2011 Editorial Report for the *Review of Higher Education* (Nora, 2011), the peer-reviewed journal of the Association for the Study of Higher Education, revealed that although 45 percent of manuscripts submitted used some sort of qualitative methodology, only 20 percent of articles accepted used qualitative methods. Whereas only 40 percent of manuscripts submitted used quantitative methods, quantitatively based studies constituted 47 percent of all accepted articles.

Furthermore, in a review of three higher education journals considered by many to be the top tier of the field, the *Journal of Higher Education*, the *Review of Higher Education,* and *Research in Higher Education*, Hutchinson and Lovell (2004) found that the majority of studies published utilized quantitative analysis (73.4 percent) and mixed methods (6.3 percent). Of the few qualitative studies published (20.3 percent), the majority were case study or generally "descriptive–qualitative." Least often published was ethnography and action research, and critical methodologies were not significant enough to be coded in Hutchinson and Lovell's study at all. In a review of the same three higher education journals, Hart (2006) found that when considering both titles and abstracts, less than 1 percent of articles included language of feminism. In-depth discussions of epistemological or ontological approach are lacking and, at times, only a brief methodological citation of a case study methodologist such as "Yin (2009)" is mentioned. As such, we argue that these journals perpetuate a status quo agenda regarding qualitative inquiry—one that narrowly defines qualitative research in accordance with dominant paradigms, methodologies, and methods. Effectively, these predominant journals promote a notion of a generic qualitative inquiry, reduced, in a sense, to the use of postpositivist case study and grounded theory methods of data collection and representation most often associated with basic thematic analyses.

We contend that such reductive and generic conceptions of qualitative research reflect the broader state of the field of qualitative research in higher education, one that does not engage deeply with philosophical assumptions that differentiate knowledge regimes, paradigms, or frameworks for their ontological, epistemological, axiological, and methodological claims. The absence of explicit discussions concerning researcher ways of knowing can reify dominant research paradigms as providing authoritative and deterministic truths—the kind of which our assumptions about the postmodern condition of global late capitalism in the twenty-first century simply refute.

And so we continue our call to arms in the name of equity and *critical* qualitative research in higher education. To put the argument plainly, dominant inquiry (including qualitative research) has failed to meet the equity claims and potential of higher education. In this chapter, we hope to illustrate this argument philosophically and materially by providing an extended discussion of the important role ontological, epistemological, axiological, and methodological assumptions play in realizing (or more frequently undermining) the equity aims of higher education scholarship. However, as criticalists, we are not cynics. Rather, we find hope in the struggle of *critical* qualitative inquiry and seek to provide some "shocks to thought" as examples of research innovations that might help dislocate the current centrifuge of power that privileges dominant post/positivist paradigms in higher education scholarship.

Beyond Method: Matters of Ontology, Epistemology, Axiology, and Methodology

Congruent with the dominant paradigms' fetishization of post/positivistic tenets of research, much of the discussion about qualitative inquiry in higher education has focused at the level of method. We argue that social change efforts do not rest in a limited choice of methods and will not succeed if they do not deal directly with issues of power, difference, and diversity within the community–university research relationships in which they operate (Ibarra, 2006; O'Connor, 2004; Rowley, 2000). Moreover, reducing qualitative inquiry to overly simplistic documentation of various data collection and analysis techniques perpetuates the objectivist notions of subjects, truth, power, and agency that have kept qualitative research in higher education from making material and systemic change toward myriad imaginations of equity. Specifically, an overfixation on method forecloses discussion of deeper philosophical assumptions out of which methods gain legitimacy. As such, issues of social justice in the name of equity cannot be addressed through research techniques and technologies but by the disruption of normative systems of meaning that make such practices possible. Consequently, we advocate against prescription of method/technique; asserting that all methods are local, contextually anchored in the specific and unique intrapersonal and interpersonal dynamics that frame inquiry; to assume otherwise is to turn researchers into technocrats.

With the assumption that cultural formations of equity are never static, we recognize three dynamically disruptive entry points for critical inquiry that extend from questions concerning the nature of reality, what can be known, and the values that undergird meaning-making. These entry points—of ontology, epistemology, and axiology, respectively—remain important areas of contestation for critical qualitative inquiry. Unfortunately, such sociocultural assumptions are rarely interrogated in the methodological literature that is most visible throughout the field of higher education. As a consequence, the potential for such scholarship to incite progressive social change concerning issues of equity is needlessly short-circuited. In response, we advocate for a critical qualitative inquiry that begins with the assumption that social justice requires new ways of being, knowing, and valuing. Our work as critical methodologists extends from an activist belief in the potential of inquiry to realize such changes. We turn next to an explication of ontology, epistemology, and axiology—what we term an *interactive triad*—specifically as they contribute to the methodological approaches of critical qualitative inquiry.

Ontology, epistemology, and axiology flow into and from each other; the terms are not entirely separable. Ontology poses the question "What is the nature of reality or being?" For example, Cartesian Dualism (1641) structures reality with a separation of the mind and body, whereas others such as Derrida (1930–2004) argue against such a dualistic approach and for a holistic nature of reality, thereby unmasking binary thinking found in Western metaphysics (Schwandt, 2007).

Epistemology asks researchers "How do you know what you know?" and is related to the origins of and assumptions about the acquisition of knowledge and justification. For example, René Descartes's concept *"cogito ergo sum"* or "I think, therefore I am" provides epistemological certainty. Further, the rationalist epistemology argues that knowledge follows from reason and in this way conceptualizes epistemology with a formal and capital "E" (Schwandt, 2007). In contrast, the perspective that researchers do the best they can based on fallible human judgment abandons the absolute and formal uppercase "E" and utilizes the lowercase "e," which reflects myriad perspectives about what it means to know (Schwandt, 2007).

Axiology asks "What is the role of values that undergird ontology and epistemology?" As such, it focuses on an ideology of ethics that informs inquiry. Some scholars also connect methodology with axiology as it invites researchers to consider "What is the process of research?" However, we assert that methodology is intimately entwined with all of these; ontological, epistemological, and axiological assumptions have methodological consequences. The qualitative inquirer would do well to strive for methodological congruency with the interactive triad of being, knowing, and valuing. Further still, the critical inquirer casts potential areas of incongruence and contradiction as important areas for interrogation.

What we describe as *methodology* has also been termed strategies of inquiry (Denzin and Lincoln, 2005a) and methodological currents of thought (Marshall and Rossman, 2011; Schram, 2006). Methodology may be defined as:

> *A theory of how inquiry should proceed. It involves analysis of the assumptions, principles, and procedures in a particular approach to inquiry (that, in turn, governs the use of particular methods). Methodologies explicate and define (a) the kinds of problems that are worth investigating, (b) what comprises a researchable problem, testable hypothesis, and so on, (c) how to frame a problem in such a way that it can be investigated using particular designs and procedures, (d) how to understand what constitutes a legitimate and warranted explanation, (e) how to judge matters of generalizability, (f) how to select or develop appropriate means of generating data, and (g) how to develop the logic linking problem - data generation - analysis - argument [Schwandt, 2007, p. 193].*

A set definition of methodology is problematic as qualitative researchers argue, for example, about whether qualitative research may ever be generalizable and if generalizability or neutrality are necessarily goals of qualitative inquiry at all and instead, simply mirror the post/positivistic paradigm from quantitative research (Denzin and Lincoln, 1994; Rosenau, 1992). Further, we would do well to interrogate the existence of *data*—a reductive term that ignores historical, sociopolitical, intercultural, and research complexities and assumes a static nature. As such, like meaning-making, qualitative inquiry is not a deterministic process: it is fragmented and forever in process where the researcher does hold some responsibility.

Subsequent methods or steps in the "data" collection and analysis process follow directly from the methodology and provide direction on the level of abstraction or concreteness of the process (Creswell, 2011b; Jones, Torres and Arminio, 2006). In this way, methodology is quite different from the term "method," which focuses on specific data collection techniques, procedures for analysis, and/or steps in the research process, albeit some researchers use these terms interchangeably. As Jones, Torres, and Arminio (2006) offer, "the assumption that simply stating the method (interview) and providing the results (analysis of themes) will lead to a thorough and worthy research process . . . is erroneous" (p. 83). Mayan (2009) echoes, "You cannot just pick and choose from any possible qualitative strategy available, throw it into the soup, and expect it to work out. This makes qualitative work sloppy and unscientific. The result is 'lousy' research" (p. 17). We might add that the overreliance on traditional post/positivist methodological approaches as a rationale for standardized research methods effectively makes inquiry docile, never able to incite constructive change in the name of social justice. To reiterate, critical qualitative research in the eighth moment (Denzin and Lincoln, 2005b) is about studying social justice and educational in/equity as well as operationalizing— or leaving intentionally vague—methodologies and methods that are reflective of a social justice perspective.

Paradigms and Worldviews

Ontology, epistemology, axiology, and methodology are also inextricably linked to a researcher's paradigms (or worldview). A paradigm or worldview provides fundamental assumptions through which you live and experience the world. Stated another way, a paradigm is what we think can be known—and how we believe we might access such knowledge, which implicates our orientation toward research; it is how we think research can and should operate within the world in which we live. Specifically, Crotty (1998) refers to a paradigm as a philosophical stance informing methodology and methods that includes positivism, constructionism, interpretivism, critical inquiry, feminism, and postmodernism. Some authors display paradigms on a continuum, from positivism to postpositivism to pragmatism (also known as symbolic interactionism) to constructivism to postmodernism to critical theory, and see the paradigms as mutually exclusive, albeit overlapping. To help new higher education researchers think through their own stance, Jones, Torres, and Arminio (2006) offer a Worldview Exercise where researchers new to qualitative inquiry consider three different perspectives that expand on three notions of reality; that reality is (1) a physical and observable event (as is found in positivism and postpositivism), (2) constructed through local human interaction (such as interpretive, constructivism, constructionism), or (3) shaped by social, political, economic, and other values established over time (subjectivism, subjectivist, and critical science). Denzin and Lincoln (2005b) echo the definition of positivist and postpositivist paradigms, yet include interpretive perspectives as inclusive of critical inquiry, ethnography, feminist discourse, critical race theory, and other critical perspectives. Further, Guba and Lincoln (2005) identify five different paradigms that make further distinctions and include positivism (reality exists), postpositivism (imperfect reality exists), critical theory (a virtual reality is shaped by historical, social, political, cultural, economic, and gender values and crystallized over time), constructivism (co-constructed realities), and participatory (participative reality where subjective and objective reality are co-created). In a different approach, Patton (2002) includes *orientational qualitative inquiry* as an umbrella term to include feminist inquiry, critical theory, critical race theory, and queer theory.

We appreciate the need to think through paradigmatic commitments, but urge higher education researchers to resist the temptation of paradigm shopping and/or obsessing over the paradigm *de jour*. Exercises like the Worldview Exercise of Jones, Torres, and Arminio (2006) may often lead to the oversimplification of paradigmatic consequences. Instead, we suggest that research paradigms are particularized yet dynamic commitments to philosophical assumptions that permeate all dimensions of qualitative inquiry, as mentioned earlier. Notably, such paradigmatic consideration may be difficult to conceptualize for higher education researchers because not all scholars agree on definitions and meanings. For example, the term *interpretivism* has been utilized as both a paradigm (in this usage it is as a synonym for all qualitative inquiry) and, more recently, a specific methodology (Schwandt, 2007). Denzin and Lincoln (1994) and Rosenau (1992) challenge traditional assumptions of neutrality in qualitative inquiry and describe all research as interpretive as it is "guided by a set of beliefs and feelings about the world and how it should be understood and studied" (Denzin and Lincoln, 1994, p. 13); and as such, objectivity and neutrality do not exist. *Phenomenology* is another paradigm that started as a multifaceted philosophy that included the transcendental phenomenology of Husserl (1859–1938), existential phenomenology of Maurice Merleau-Ponty (1908–1961) and Jean-Paul Sartre (1905–1980), and hermeneutic phenomenology of Heidegger (1889–1976;

Schwandt, 2007). When Husserl (1931, 1970) coined the term, he intended that phenomenology was the study of how people describe things and experience them through their senses. More recently fashioned into a methodology (Moustakas, 1994; van Manen, 1990), this constructivist approach asks researchers to uncover the lived experience of participants or the essence of what people experience. Another example of alternate meanings, the term *postmodernity* refers to a socio-historical context or condition, and *postmodernism* refers to a research paradigm with simultaneous experiences and realities. Yet, even this notion is contested as it places postmodernism in opposition to modernism, where modernism is erroneously centered as "it represents a reaction to, critique of, or departure from modernism" (Schwandt, 2007, p. 235; also see Best and Kellner, 1991, or Butler, 2002). It remains important to note that multiple definitions by different scholars at different moments in history add to the complexity, ambiguity, and dynamic nature of qualitative inquiry. Such paradigmatic approaches to qualitative inquiry reveal assumptions about our social and political world.

As mentioned, all aspects of a researcher's philosophical approach (ontology, epistemology, axiology, paradigm, methodology, and methods) are connected. They build upon and inform each other—they exist in dynamic interrelation. As such, research cannot be conducted without conscious or unconscious use of underlying theoretical principles (Broido and Manning, 2002). Even studies that read as void of theoretical underpinnings actually enact some semblance of philosophical and theoretical principles; it is not possible to be void of theoretical underpinnings. Conscious or unconscious, these philosophical assumptions are inextricably linked to the approach a researcher takes in any research process and as such, a scholar may perpetuate dominant research paradigms or seek to disrupt them. (For more on conscious/unconscious dimensions, see Hardiman and Jackson, 2007.) Recognized and intentional paradigmatic perspectives may help researchers clearly conceptualize their approach to the study as well as render issues of in/equity, ethics, power, and politics visible in the research process. Left unacknowledged, higher education researchers perpetuate a hidden research agenda, one that remains unclear to audiences, and, at times, to themselves (Pasque, forthcoming). As mentioned in the first chapter of this monograph, hidden agendas stemming from unrecognized paradigms often manifest as dangers to social justice, especially when such an unconscious paradigm is built from contradictory philosophical, theoretical, and methodological assumptions.

The Promise and Hope of Critical Qualitative Inquiry

As discussed in the previous chapter and elaborated upon earlier in this chapter, we argue that dominant traditions of qualitative inquiry fail to address the fundamental philosophical underpinnings of in/equity in higher education. Participatory action research, critical inquiry, and other forms of social justice qualitative research problematize the cycle of socialization, incorporate marginalized voices within the research processes, and make visible alternative paradigms. In the past, theorists within the fields of feminist and cultural studies have rightly drawn our attention to issues of power, reflexivity, and positionality in order to address the silencing of underrepresented groups. Such work reminds us that the ways in which we represent the participants of our studies and ourselves as researchers within our studies matters. Naming the gaps and theoretical inconsistencies in our research perspectives and practice can have serious implications on our capacity to effect educational change, allowing scholars to actively confront and resist the silences around their own ideologies. As Lather (2003) argues, we need "emancipatory theory-building through the development of interactive and action-inspiring research designs" (p. 186). Critical qualitative inquiry is one such option.

Although the critical tradition resists the articulation of a universal definition (Kincheloe and McLaren, 2005), our understanding of critical inquiry is guided by a set of distinct philosophical assumptions and scholarly principles. These assumptions include an understanding of oppression as a multifaceted phenomenon reproduced through the acceptance of domination and subordination as inevitable features of modern society; the recognition that data and evidence framed as objective fact within "scientific" educational research are indeed reflections of dominant societal values and political ideologies; and agreement with Kincheloe and McLaren (2005) that "mainstream research practices are generally, although often unwittingly, implicated in the reproduction of systems of class, race and gender oppression" (p. 304; also see

Cannella and Lincoln, 2009). For the purposes of this chapter, we focus on this last principle—the recognition that research is a political and often imperial act that contributes to the continued oppression of historically marginalized individuals and communities (Cannella and Lincoln, 2004b). Rather than continue to be implicated in the perpetuation of repressive research norms, critical higher education scholars seek to enact methodological principles and practices that realize the transformational potential of inquiry—research as a vehicle of resistance (Brown and Strega, 2005) and activism which contributes to real, material change in the lives of those most touched by inequitable power relations in our society (Cannella and Lincoln, 2009).

Although certainly not an exhaustive list, examples of decolonizing qualitative methodological perspectives include participatory action research (Brydon-Miller and others, 2011; McIntyre, 2008), performance ethnography (Barad, 2008; Denzin, 2003), arts-based inquiry (Finley, 2011; Norris, 2009), critical ethnography (Foley and Valenzuela, 2005; Gildersleeve, 2010; Madison, 2011; Valenzuela, 1999), Indigenous methodologies (Battiste, 2008; Brown and Strega, 2005; Smith, 1999; Wilson and Yellow Bird, 2005), autoethnography (Guido, 2011; Reed-Danahay, 1997; Spry, 2011), and counter-storytelling (Solórzano and Delgado Bernal, 2001; Solórzano and Yosso, 2002). We contend that critical methodological perspectives such as these are well suited for studying, and more important remedying, issues of educational inequity given that these "politically radical research paradigms" (Anyon, 2006, p. 24–25) emphasize working *with* historically marginalized individuals and communities to document, publicize, and resist oppressive conditions that contribute to discriminatory educational environments and outcomes. In addition, examining and resolving issues of inequity necessitates acknowledging the tangled web of political, economic, social, historical, and cultural factors that create and reinscribe repressive power regimes (Anyon, 2006). Accordingly, critical scholars place at the center of inquiry the multidimensional nature of oppression, exploring the intersecting influences of public policy, family, social identities, geography, global political instability, human trafficking, warfare, and so on, on the experiences, opportunities, and achievements of historically underrepresented groups in higher education.

To effect change through qualitative research is, admittedly, no easy task. As the field of higher education continues to grow, it remains vital that scholars continually investigate the absences and invisibilities inherent in dominant research paradigms and explore the transformative possibilities embedded in critical epistemological and methodological perspectives. We take up this conversation, turning our attention to innovations in qualitative research. Specifically, building on the introduction to critical inquiry presented above, we explore the important role critical qualitative inquiry may play in advancing the equity aims of contemporary higher education scholarship. Drawing upon the emergent critical scholarship on inquiry for social change, we next foreground methodological possibilities as they extend from disruptions to normative conceptions of being and knowing.

Innovation as Research Revolutions

It is our claim that innovations in inquiry that focus on the social justice issues inherent in discussions regarding equity necessarily bring about change at the level of ontology and epistemology, and are interrelated to axiology and methodology. As noted earlier, discussions regarding innovative research practices fixate all too frequently on the specter of method, as though alterations to specialized techniques of research alone will bring about shifts in how we understand ourselves in relation to others, or draw new awareness to previously absent voices and identities within higher education scholarship. It is our hope in this text to change such thinking—to challenge readers to resist simplistic notions of innovative methods in favor of more epistemological and ontological concerns, and to do so in the name of equity and inquiry for social justice in higher education. In many ways, our call is a movement toward a more revolutionary perspective on inquiry and away from reformist claims for change at the level of method.

Before considering particular innovative methodological orientations and practices, it makes sense to revisit the very notion of innovation. The *Oxford English Dictionary*'s definition of the noun *innovation* includes "the alteration of what is established by the introduction of new elements or forms" as well as "revolution" and "a rebellion or insurrection." All too often, notions of innovation in methodological discussions emphasize the former consideration of "new elements or forms" at the expense of concerns regarding revolution, rebellion, or insurrection. An overemphasis on new particulars in qualitative inquiry most often results in a fixation on the creation of new methodological techniques, strategies for acquiring and coding qualitative data. Though it remains important to locate emergent methods in qualitative inquiry, alterations in the form of inquiry—inquiry as method—do little to address such fundamental issues such as equity and resistance in educational research. Importantly, assertions regarding research techniques, no matter how innovative, rarely influence change at the level of epistemology—in this case innovation remains tangled at the level of method. If progressive change is to occur through inquiry, it necessarily must take place at the very systems of logic—that is ontology, epistemology, and axiology—that inform a qualitative approach to inquiry. Unfortunately, few scholars—in the field of higher education as well as other social sciences—recognize the radical elements of innovation when dealing with methodology. A ten-year review (2000–2009) of an interdisciplinary array of methodology-specific journals found that the majority of 57 articles surveyed presented small adaptations to existing methodologies as "innovative" and few presented new ways of thinking through approaches to inquiry (Wiles, Pain, and Crow, 2010).

As an example of innovations at the level of method versus more radical conceptions of innovation in the realm of methodology, consider the example of grounded theory, which is an extremely common qualitative methodological approach in the field of education (second only to case study as found by Hutchinson and Lovell, 2004). Thomas and James (2006) assert that grounded theory has become so popular in social science and educational research because it meets a need: it provides researchers direction, a set of procedures, and a prescribed means for generating a theory. The authors question the assumed legitimacy of the approach as well as its "lofty place" in contemporary qualitative scholarship (p. 768). After reviewing a series of assumptions regarding the intersection of grounded theory with a variety of paradigmatic positions, the authors critique Charmaz's (2000) claim that grounded theory is consistent with a constructivist approach. They note that Charmaz's approach (as well as her determination to reinvoke the term *grounded theory*) undermines alternative approaches to qualitative inquiry, placing "unwelcome constraints on open, creative interpretation" of data inherent in the research process.

In more specific relation to our work in this chapter, Thomas and James (2006) note the grounded theory approach—both in its forced design and the cultural contexts in which it is privileged—constrains the more radical conceptions of innovation in inquiry even as it legitimizes more palatable assertions of innovation at the level of method. They go on to write, "continued allegiance to grounded theory procedures—or, strangely, loyalty simply to the term 'grounded theory,' unstitched from its procedures or putative ends—stunts and distorts the growth of qualitative inquiry" (p. 790). As such, Thomas and James advocate for the rejection of grounded theory as a residue of post/positivism and call for more creative—innovative—approaches to qualitative inquiry.

What, then, does methodological innovation look like—how might it be understood—when brought to bear on questions of equity and methodological responsibility? As a necessary consequence, methodological innovations alter perspectives on the world; they do not simply extend previously held beliefs or social assumptions.

As asserted in the previous chapter, equity involves considerations of an ongoing array of social processes and institutions and their subsequent impact on select social groups; the ways in which such social arrangements disadvantage some groups and legitimate others. Considerations for equity call forth issues of justness and fairness as well as strategies aimed at accounting for historical lineages of inequality (Chomsky, 2004; Giroux, 2001; Giroux and Giroux, 2004; Young, 1990, 2010). Unfortunately, issues of equity rarely make their way into methodological discussions or, if they are addressed, such discussions inevitably remain at the level of method—those techniques aimed at accounting for or documenting the production of inequitable circumstance.

Through our discussion of innovation, issues of fairness and justice are not divorced from methodology—they are, instead, highlighted and folded within such important discussions. Further, methodological innovations might be seen as particular strategies for intervention in the very production of the status quo—how we make sense of the world in which we live. Innovation then, can be understood as shocks to thought, challenges to how we make meaning, requiring a shift in the very system of logics that produce our common sense. As a consequence, methodological innovation remains implicitly driven by ontological and epistemological concerns about the social world. Such assumptions reveal themselves in the very methodological choices that govern our studies. Innovations such as these, we believe, can provide revolutionary researches that might affect material social change for equity.

Epistemology and Critical Qualitative Work

The critical turn in inquiry foregrounds and extends concerns specifically regarding epistemological assumptions of positioning. These concerns stem from the recognition that we live in newly emergent times, with multiple interpretations of reality. These contexts have prompted a critical reassessment of epistemological assumptions in an interdisciplinary array of fields. As Marcus and Fischer (1999) note, "the most interesting theoretical debates in a number of fields have shifted to the level of method, to problems of epistemology" (p. 9). Note here how Marcus and Fischer assume a direct connection between "the level of method" and "problems of epistemology." The critical turn out of which Marcus and Fischer operate requires such a conjoined relation between the two concepts; one cannot exist without the other. Though it is beyond the scope of this chapter to provide a full treatment of the epistemic, a brief overview follows in order to better frame the rationalities that undergird the methodological innovations offered later in this chapter.

Thomas Schwandt (1999) notes that, as a field of study, qualitative inquiry remains "deeply concerned with fundamentally epistemological matters" (p. 463). In this sense, qualitative inquiry has a long history of considering theories of knowledge—ways of knowing and coming to know. The critical turn in qualitative inquiry questioned the limits of traditional knowledge structures, the assumptions they make about the knower, the known, and the contexts in which knowing happens. Specific to issues of inquiry in education, Cynthia Dillard (2000) asks for a shift at the level of epistemology "if educational research is to truly change or transform" (p. 663). As such, scholars invested in working toward social change through educational research assert that transformation must necessarily begin with epistemological shifts, that is, with counter-claims to traditional theories of knowledge. Contemporary innovations in qualitative inquiry have sought to incorporate methodological approaches and practices that extend from revised epistemological assumptions, new ways of knowing that counter the claims of post/positivism.

In response to traditional epistemological claims regarding holistic knowledge and quests toward accessing universal truths (seen in post/positivistic forms of scholarship), critical qualitative scholars foreground relational ways of knowing and coming to know even as they maintain an emphasis on the social and material contexts in which knowledges form. An excellent example of this might be found in the work of Michael Gunzenhauser (2006) who, through assertions of critical qualitative inquiry, lays claim to the relationships between the researcher and participant as "simultaneously epistemological and ethical" (p. 622). The key to a critical perspective, for Gunzenhauser, is a shift from a knower–known relation between researcher and participant to a more critically aligned epistemological relation of "two knowing subjects" (p. 627). Strategically, then, the qualitative inquirer immerses him/hir/herself[2] within the multiple contexts of the research study, acting as a co-constructer of knowledge alongside research participants: "Immersion and emergence are epistemological hallmarks of qualitative research for researchers who adopt any number of interpretivist or critical theoretical perspectives" (p. 624). Yet, as noted early in this chapter, such immersion is aimed not at reproducing but intervening within traditional representations of the status quo. If we follow Gunzenhauser's system of logic, we recognize that "two knowing subjects" can never simply render the same interpretation of some objective reality (the sense of qualitative research as simplistically descriptive and identifies a truth)— instead, they both work to co-create newly emergent understandings of the world in which we live as well as their own interconnected processes of meaning-making.

Moreover, Wright (2003) notes the critical shift in epistemology as working against the specter of a "cohesive subject." No longer is inquiry set on accessing an objective reality, nor the fully known subject, both residues of post/positivism. Critical inquiry does not set out to achieve complete knowing of individual subjects or social processes. Instead, critical inquiry recognizes individuals as fragmented, produced through the intersection of multiple (and, at times, contradictory) social processes. In a similar manner, the researcher is also fragmented and produced through intersections of sociopolitical processes and contexts. Thus, "knowing the subject" is less emphasized in critical work than coming to know the historical discourses in which such subjects are immersed as well as reflecting on researcher reflexivity (as will be discussed in more detail in the final chapter).

Further, critical qualitative work operates from a logic formation that refutes deterministic thinking, most often articulated through traditional cause-and-effect rationalities. Thus, Somerville (2007) turns to a postmodern epistemological stance, one that "fundamentally addresses the question of causation, profoundly challenging the empiricist model of the linked determinism of cause and effect" (p. 237). In this way, critical qualitative inquiry challenges traditional assertions of empiricism as necessarily governed by the principles of the scientific method, involving elements of predicting particular causes which in turn produce subsequent effects. What might inquiry look like if it were to operate outside deterministic rationalities and epistemological assumptions of causation?

Somerville (2007) notes that challenges to deterministic ways of knowing require a simultaneous need for a new vision of representation, one that "embraces multiple modes of expression, such as stories, song, dance and paintings, as well as interviews, academic prose and so on" (p. 239). Somerville thus foregrounds a methodological stance bent on emergent and context specific methodologies, an assemblage of representation. It is out of these primary concerns that innovation in qualitative inquiry begins. In order to ground Somerville's comments and as a means for illuminating specific innovations in qualitative inquiry, we focus on those approaches that foreground material and embodied contexts, as well as multivocal and performative means for communicating the impact of inquiry to others. We use these innovations as they stem from a theoretical counter to traditionally held values of Cartesian duality and researcher power formations, respectively. Such innovations seek a disruptive impact not only on the daily production of inquiry, but the commonsensical processes of meaning-making that legitimize such activity. In short, these innovative approaches to inquiry seek altered practices through epistemological (re)formations.

Dialogue as Insurrection

As an example, consider the notion of dialogue as an epistemological innovation within the realm of inquiry that takes seriously the co-constructive nature of "two knowing subjects." Within their text *Breaking Bread: Insurgent Black Intellectual Life,* hooks and West (1991) offer a series of dialogues as inquiry into a host of contemporary issues regarding race, class, gender, feminism, and intellectual work, to name but a few. Equally as important, however, is the authors' use of dialogue to make visible the process through which they come to know and communicate that meaning to one another. In important ways, dialogue exists in this text as a means for inquiry; one that does not adhere to traditional notions of objective claims of knowledge or knowledge production.

In the same vein, Gildersleeve and Kuntz (2011) offer dialogue as a dynamic means of inquiry when considering the impact of space on higher education scholarship. Through their use of dialogue, the authors present a "mapping out of [their] ideas" that is, itself, spatial (p. 16). In this way, Gildersleeve and Kuntz offer dialogue as a method that inherently demonstrates the very processes they seek to describe. Further, the process of dialogue offers both hooks and West as well as Gildersleeve and Kuntz a means for resisting the temptation of simplistic articulations of consensus in their inquiry process. (Also see Walker and Zinn, 2010/1996). In this sense, dialogue foregrounds disagreement and dissensus over traditional claims of synthesis and unification of ideas or points of view. Dialogue makes visible the contradictory nature of meaning-making in relation, foregrounding the very differences that post/positivistic ways of knowing and coming to know often seek to overcome. Thus, knowledge is represented through its fragmentary production; a consideration that extends to figurations of fragmented individuals and identities, both elements that emerge from the critical turn in qualitative inquiry. Dialogue as a methodological approach intersects with a transformative epistemological stance, one that refuses traditionally held relations of the knower to the known. As a methodological innovation, dialogue here intervenes, disrupting claims for static ways of knowing and coming to know.

Revolutionary Subjects

In seeking to counter or otherwise intervene within traditional epistemological assertions, it seems important to recognize the non-innocence of seemingly commonsensical or "clear" conclusions of what can be known and how we might access such knowledge. This position of willful doubt extends from Foucault's

(1984) famous axiom that nothing is innocent and everything is dangerous, which we discussed in the first chapter. Of course, Foucault (1997) followed up on this assertion by noting "my point is not that everything is bad, but that everything is dangerous, which is not exactly the same as bad. If everything is dangerous then we always have something to do" (p. 256). Thus, it remains important to interrogate our seemingly intuited understandings of the world as well as the system of rationalities that make such understandings possible. In this sense, the critical qualitative inquirer who takes seriously questions of in/equity and social justice, "always has something to do."

More contemporary innovations in qualitative inquiry have taken seriously the problems associated with Cartesian Duality, or the separation of mind from body. Cartesian Duality privileges the mind at the expense of the body, as well as other material contexts, and has become naturalized as an everyday way of knowing and coming to know; on many levels in our contemporary culture, Cartesian Duality "just makes sense." Methodologically, contemporary theorists, including indigenous theorists, have sought to disrupt the legitimization of the mind-body split through working with the material world generally, and issues regarding emplacement and embodiment more specifically.

In the field of education, this mind–body split can be seen in assertions of "proper education" occurring when students sit quietly in desks, ignoring the "distractions" of their own bodies and those surrounding them, as well as the erasure of physical education classes and outdoor play time or recess for students across the country. This continues in higher education as colleges and universities most often replicate bodies in chairs, chairs screwed stationary into the floor, erasing opportunities for movement with innovative teaching and learning pedagogies, and education as acting upon the mind. More directly, the overemphasis of the mind at the expense of the body in higher education causes bell hooks (1993) to note its implications on her everyday teaching practices in the collegiate classroom:

> When I first became a teacher and needed to use the restroom in the middle of class, I had no clue as to what my elders did in such situations. No one talked about the body in relation to teaching.

What did one do with the body in the classroom? Trying to remember the bodies of my professors, I find myself unable to recall them. I hear voices, remember fragmented details but very few whole bodies [p. 58].

hooks offers a poignant recognition of the absence of the body in educational discussions, resulting in an intuited hesitancy when forced to recognize her own body in the collegiate classroom: "What did one do with the body in the classroom?" Importantly, the mind–body split impacts hooks at the level of daily practice; it is more than a simple theoretical division. Similarly, we might shift hooks' observations to the problematic of inquiry—given the historical imposition of the distinct separation of mind from body—"what does one do with the body in the research process?" If we continue to give epistemological primacy to minds-without-bodies we run the risk of recognizing the body only when it is marked by difference; such bodies conveniently made visible in our research on account of their deviance. This overemphasis of the deviant in relation to the historically normalized and legitimated body has significant consequences for issues regarding equity and social justice in higher education scholarship. What bodies are visible in our minds when we consider issues such as access to higher education? What bodies are rendered invisible in such formations? What nonverbal behaviors from bodies are reified or ostracized in college contexts?

This normalization of select bodily representations, the corresponding absence of other bodies, as well as the privileging of the mind as the conduit through which education occurs, causes Ryan Gildersleeve to note:

Migrant students know more about labor practices, capitalism, neocolonialism, and educational opportunity than most anthropology professors at elite universities. They know it in their bodies, rather than articulate it through their cognitive sense-making communiqués [Gildersleeve and Kuntz, 2011, p. 19].

Gildersleeve's assertions thus present a methodological quandary for researchers well schooled in the logics of Cartesian Duality—how to attend to bodies and places, to render visible the very elements one has been trained to overlook? Such questions require epistemological revisions and methodological innovations on the part of the inquirer.

Poststructural Voices

St. Pierre (1997) articulates the shift away from Cartesian Duality as a historical transformation from the *humanist subject* to an emergent *poststructural subjectivity*. The *humanist subject* emphasizes a complete, static subject that, in turn, establishes a clear sense of internal and external (a division that separates the individual from the multiple contexts in which s/z/he is immersed). This static subject demonstrates a strong sense of self-definition and determination (I know who I am; I have a core internal self that remains unchanged regardless of time or space). In order to understand the consequences of traditional uses of the *humanist subject,* we might recognize particular "subjects" that are privileged and rendered more legitimate over time. Such subjects are often romanticized in contemporary culture in terms of what it means to be a man, woman, transgender, or even a citizen in our society.

Poststructural subjectivity, on the other hand, "is without a centered essence that remains the same throughout time" (St. Pierre, 1997, p. 5), and is produced through multiple (and often contradictory) discourses. This shift away from the *humanist subject* requires a simultaneous rejection of traditional rationalities that seek "true" knowledge of "authentic" selves.

The recognition of a *poststructural subjectivity* presents a new ethical imperative to "think differently than we have thought" (St. Pierre, 1997, p. 2), to think as other than we have been trained to think, to consider newly possible interpretations of the world in which we live. St. Pierre asks the critical inquirer to think outside the language of humanism, what she deems our "mother tongue" and has resulted in traditionally static categories, binaries, and structures that potentially keep us all—not to mention the participants who collaborate in our inquiries—tied to the deterministic lines of thought that remain emblematic of post/positivism. Thinking outside of humanism requires the methodologist to participate in "getting free of oneself" (p. 2). Again, it remains important to note that working outside of humanism requires a deep sense of change, more than can be achieved through simple innovations at the level of method. Scholars influenced by the philosophy of Deleuze, such as Brian Massumi (2002), consider this a "shock to thought." As St. Pierre notes, traditional methodological approaches do little to free oneself from humanism, most often resulting in the reification of the *humanist subject*.

We next follow St. Pierre's insights to recognize their impact on qualitative inquiry practices. St. Pierre's (1997) assertion that qualitative inquiry must necessarily move away from the humanist subject to conceptions of poststructural subjectivity calls to question other essentialized methodological issues such as voice, a primary concern for Jackson and Mazzei (2009). Too often, Jackson and Mazzei note, voice is asked to stand in for the humanist subject, understood to represent a unified self, one that upholds traditional hierarchies between the researcher and researched. Like the traditionally romanticized claims of the humanist subject, *voice* in qualitative inquiry has come to occupy a privileged position throughout the research process. We seek purity of voice, an unobstructed, clear articulation of voice in our research articles that adheres to standardized retellings of the research process, procedures, and findings.

Far too often, our attention to the (re)presentation of some authorial voice recreates humanist subjects and does little to disrupt unified and static subject formations. As such, critical qualitative inquirers should remain rightly skeptical of claims for methodological and epistemological "transparency"—there remains nothing transparent about truth-telling (further, as Jackson and Mazzei go on to note, there is nothing unproblematic about transparency). Thus, Jackson and Mazzei (2009) assert the incompatibility of contemporary epistemological positions and methodological claims for complete understanding: "Poststructural theory rejects the presence of an experience that can be fully understood and that can be directly expressed through reflection" (p. 302). In this sense, assertions of what they term the "narrative-I" become ethical questions; the requirement of taking the critical turn in qualitative inquiry seriously. As a consequence, critical qualitative inquiry must necessarily interrogate its own claims for truth as well as learned tendencies toward constructing a unified voice out of often divergent and contradictory interpretations of the social world. Pasque (2010a) speaks to the poststructural critique of imagined unity in her observation that policy reports in higher education contexts often serve as a strategy to show consensus, whether present or not. Indeed, meaning-making is a complex and often messy process—we might rightly remain skeptical of renderings that oversimplify such processes through the articulation of a coherent and identifiable narrative "I."

This ethical requirement of resisting the urge for epistemological unification or clarity is further addressed in Patti Lather's (2007) *Getting Lost: Feminist Efforts Towards a Double(d) Science.* Lather presents a critique of her earlier (1995) ethnographic work through questioning attempts to contain the "wholly other" through research practices. In response, Lather asks inquirers to interrogate claims toward "clear speech," to consider the "violence of clarity, its non-innocence" (p. 86). Like Jackson and Mazzei's (2009) interrogation of transparency, Lather alludes to clarity as a violent strategy, one that brings with it a host of power relations bent on forcing a particularly "clear" interpretation of reality on others. Such clarity assumes that singular objects exist, can be fully known, and might be fully articulated or communicated to others. Against such assertions of clarity, Lather asks the critical inquirer to trouble the very categories s/z/he cannot do without—what it means to "have evidence" or "know something" or "present your case" for some particular finding or assertion. Thus, Lather looks not for new knowledges, but new ways of coming to know, and that which resists complete definition. In this sense, Lather asks the critical inquirer to begin from an epistemological position of excess, of knowledge as forever escaping complete representation. There is always more that escapes the interpretive eye—excess spills over, eluding methodological capture. Here, the notion of excess resists complete definition; resists being confined to elements of "clear speech," even as it provokes commonsensical ways of knowing and coming to know. Lather thus presents her readers with a methodological positioning of "getting lost"—of resisting the urge to retrace the hardened pathway of previous knowledges.

In this sense, all methodological renderings fail to fully capture that which they seek to describe. Yet, as themselves examples of "getting lost," away from the pull of the commonsensical or the traditionally known, such articulations might be read as productive failures; a falling short that makes possible newly emergent epistemological positionings.

To return to Foucault's (1984) assertion that "everything is dangerous"— a sentiment that began in the introduction and was further explored in this section—it is the well-worn path of legitimated knowledges and clearly artic-ulated rationalities that inflict violence and are most dangerous to the critical inquirer, thus leaving him/her/hir with an endless array of things to do. The critical inquirer must step outside the humanist frame to dwell in the excesses of our postmodern time.

Spatial and Embodied Innovations

We end this chapter by pointing to two particular methodological strategies and innovations that draw from larger-ordered epistemological concerns with Cartesian Duality and other traditionally legitimized ways of knowing and coming to know. These perspectives emphasize the role of embodiment and emplacement, respectively, as well as their corresponding intervention within traditional epistemological formations.

To begin, Kuntz (2009) has criticized scholarship on higher education as hesitant to take seriously the "spatial turn" inherent in the postmodern experi-ence. Higher education scholarship has overly relied on temporal formations of knowledge, most often represented through progressively linear represen-tations of coming to know. As Kuntz notes, all too often,

> *Higher education research employs temporal frameworks: develop-mental models for students and faculty, narrative accounts of iden-tity development, positivist characterizations of human behavior along fixed trajectories, and neoclassical economic analyses of effi-ciency [p. 355].*

To counter such temporal formations, Kuntz points to the promise of crit-ical geography as producing innovative approaches to inquiry with implica-tions at the level of epistemology and methodology. Prominently placed within the field of critical geography is the work of Edward Soja (1989, 1996, 2000) and Doreen Massey (1996, 2005); the combination of their work offers much in the way of shifting habitual reliances on the temporal toward a more process-based understanding of the spatial.

Soja emphasizes the dailyness of spatial ways of knowing; the means by which space emphasizes the intersection of social processes and everyday practices. Thus,

Soja makes it a point to emphasize "the space in which we actually live, where history grates on us and erodes our lives, a space of complete experience, of the unseen and incomprehensible as well as the tangible and the everyday" (Blake, 2002, p. 141). For Soja (1989), the spatial realm remains important to postmodern positionalities, existing "as a product of a transformational process" that is never fixed, remaining "open to further transformation in the context of material life. [Space] is never primordially given or permanently fixed" (p. 122).

Massey (1996) echoes Soja, connecting the incessant transformative processes of space with the dynamic qualities of social relations. Thus, we exist ontologically in an ongoing array of intersecting and transforming spaces, steeped in a series of dynamic social relations. We must thus strive to establish epistemological ways of knowing that account for such transformative possibilities; a system of coming to know that dwells in simultaneity and is no longer reliant on developmental trajectories of knowledge acquisition. Practically speaking, Massey "emphasizes that social groups and identities occupy different spatial locations within the microgeographies of everyday life" (Kuntz, 2009, p. 378).

These spatial locales are inherently political, with some recognized and legitimated at the expense of others. Inherently, then, critical geography and its interrogation of spatial emplacements remains concerned with issues of equity and social justice—what spaces come to matter and what sorts of people come to inhabit such mattering spaces? For example, in his discussion on New Orleans, Louisiana disaster, hope, and education, Gildersleeve (2011) reflected:

> In our increasingly globalized societies of today, it is easy to recognize some disasters: the Rwandan genocide of the 1990's, the 2011 earthquake, tsunami and subsequent nuclear crisis in Japan, and of course, in 2005, Hurricane Katrina on the Gulf Coast. These are [spatial] disasters that can be named, codified, and recorded as historical events. Within these disasters-as-events, characters emerge. Some are etched in our minds as heroes. Others as villains. Disasters-as-events also produce responses, which become ensnared as part of the event-as-drama and build our social narrative that further solidifies these characters in our consciousness. But there is another form of disaster—disaster as process, as system, as cartography of

inequity and dehumanization. These disasters often go unnoticed, unnamed, and escape social scrutiny. Disaster-as-system of inequality produces characters as well, but they are more fluid, less-tangible, and vacillate nearly freely between our discursive productions and material [spatial] experiences, masking them as aloof, not-quite-sure senses of something being not-quite-right or even downright wrong, depending on where we might find ourselves becoming etched into the cartographies of disaster.

As Gildersleeve points out, the dehumanization of bodies that accompany each disaster reifies manifestations of hierarchies, power, privilege, and oppression. In addition, Gildersleeve describes disaster as process, as system, as cartography (or in our case, epistemology, methodology, and methods) where these intangibles matter—yet often go unnoticed or unnamed; the material space and discursive/intangible space are intertwined. Yet, methodological innovations of critical geography in higher education are often ignored. Within scholarship in the field of higher education, a shift to the spatial might reconfigure our understanding of who comes to occupy privileged positions on college and university campuses worldwide, and, more importantly, begs the question: What spaces and occupants are included or disregarded through such roles and occupations? Unfortunately, higher education scholarship in the United States has been slow to embrace such dynamic interpretations of the spatial.

In the United Kingdom, Paul Temple (2008, 2009) has worked to foreground the spatial in higher education. Specifically, Temple (2009) asks for sustained inquiry into "how space becomes place, and how it affects the work of the institution" (p. 212). Recognizing that spatial studies in tertiary education represent a "methodologically difficult area" Temple (2008) emphasizes the need for greater sensitivity to the intersections of the spatial and academic work practices (p. 238).

Hand-in-hand with questions of the spatial and issues surrounding emplacement come innovative perspectives that stem from critical interrogations of embodied knowledges. Within the realm of inquiry, critique that extends from an embodied perspective points to qualitative researchers' overreliance on language, or the linguistic, absent the material import of our bodies. This fixation on linguistic modes of meaning-making has caused scholars such as Barad (2008) to ask, "How did language come to be more trustworthy than matter?" (p. 120). The emphasis on the discursive at the expense of the material mistakenly assumes that the two are distinct, bifurcated with many of the same results as Cartesian Duality. Indeed, the discursive-materialist binary remains emblematic of the same divisional rationalities that govern formations of Cartesian Duality. This is to say that discursive formations are all too often read absent their material effects and, conversely, the material and embodied realm is rendered distinct from socially discursive processes of meaning-making.

Additionally, the absence of the body in our educational inquiries allows for a distancing of the researcher, a (mis)recognition that researcher and participant bodies no longer matter. Thus, the use of the interview in qualitative research, for example, abstracts language-as-data from the material and embodied contexts in which such utterances were spoken. This leads Brinkmann (2011) to assert, "too many interviews today are conducted based on . . . a spectator's stance—a voyeur's epistemology or an epistemology of the eye" (p. 59). The privilege of the researcher to remain a spectator (and a disembodied spectator at that) reinscribes the very inequitable power formations in which critical qualitative inquiry seeks to intervene. As critical scholars intent on pursuing social justice in higher education research we cannot afford to abide by traditional epistemological formations that privilege the separation of bodies from minds, material conditions from discursive renderings, nor claims for holistic subjects and complete knowledge formations. Thus, we find promise in scholars such as Sara Pink (2009), whose work on sensory ethnographies foreground the emplaced and embodied nature of interviews. As Pink writes:

> In interviews, researchers participate or collaborate with research participants in the process of defining and representing their (past, present, or imagined) emplacement and their sensory embodied experiences. If we situate the interview within a process through which experiences are constituted, it might be understood as a point in this process where multisensorial experience is verbalized through culturally constructed sensory categories and in the context of the intersubjective interaction between ethnographer and research participant [p. 85].

Here, the interview is caught up in a vast array of social processes, implicated by the dynamic qualities of embodied and emplaced activities. In this sense, interviews do not seek to capture "authentic retrospective experiences" but instead are understood as the very processes "through which experiences are constituted" and intersubjectivities are made known. Pink provides an excellent example of a particular research technique (in this case the interview) as inherently implicated by epistemological innovation. Once we accept new ways of coming to know, newly epistemic formations of knowledge, we necessarily alter the very methods that have traditionally been privileged in qualitative inquiry. These are the types of innovative changes we seek in critical qualitative inquiry, particularly those lines of research that take into account questions of equity and social justice within the emergent field of higher education.

Concluding Thoughts

In this chapter we offer the unrealized possibility for inquiry to change the very ways in which we live, know, and come to value. As criticalists, we advocate for interrogations that extend beyond the simplistic question of method. As such, we promote innovation in qualitative inquiry as radical activity, pointing to alterations to the traditional epistemologies that most often escape critical notice. An important innovation extends from critiques of Cartesian Duality, a mind–body split that continues to influence our commonsensical formations of meaning-making, or what Althusser (1971) termed *know-how*. We continue this dialogue on methodological innovations in equity-oriented higher education scholarship in the next chapter, turning our attention to the challenges and opportunities associated with conducting critical qualitative inquiry in the contemporary era of methodological conservatism. Specifically, we examine the increasing dominance of two inextricably connected disciplining discourse regimes—academic capitalism and scientifically based educational research—and take up the question, "What is at stake for both historically marginalized communities and critical qualitative higher education scholars if dominant post/positivist methodological perspectives continue to frame the principles and practices of higher education inquiry?"

.

Critical Concerns for Qualitative Inquiry in Higher Education

IN THIS CHAPTER WE EXPLORE several methodological concerns of relevance to higher education scholars seeking to examine and address issues of in/equity via critical qualitative methodological perspectives. Specifically, we draw upon qualitative inquiry scholarship produced within and beyond the boundaries of the higher education research community to call attention to important methodological dialogues shaping (and in many cases constraining) the nature, scope, and future of critical qualitative inquiry. It is not our intention to present an exhaustive list of methodological tensions confronting critical qualitative higher education scholars; this is an impossible task given the recent proliferation of qualitative methodological perspectives and approaches (Cannella and Lincoln, 2007; Denzin, 2009) as well as the multitude of issues that must be considered when designing and engaging in qualitative research (for example, access to people and/or spaces, rapport with participants, positionality, representation, reflexivity, ethical behavior, data analysis, qualitative research represented as text, and so on—the list is endless). A number of informative texts provide both broad overviews and deep discussions of foundational qualitative methodological considerations (for example, Creswell, 2007; Denzin and Lincoln, 1994, 2000, 2005b, 2011; Jones, Torres and Arminio, 2006; Marshall and Rossman, 2011; Maxwell, 2004; Merriam, 2009; Patton, 2002). Rather than repeat methodological insights well documented within and across multiple qualitative inquiry handbooks, in this chapter we seek to extend the dialogue on qualitative research within the higher education scholarly community by addressing what we perceive to be a substantial gap in the literature—an examination of the origins and manifestations of contemporary methodological conservatism (Denzin and Giardina, 2006; Lincoln and Cannella, 2004a, 2004b) within postsecondary research and the implication of this movement for critical qualitative scholars.

Despite the growing bodies of scholarship on the social justice aims, principles, and practices of critical qualitative inquiry, these methodological perspectives remain muted and marginalized within the higher education research community. We view the hesitancy of higher education scholars to engage with or employ critical methodologies as symptomatic of larger social processes at work within and beyond the academy—namely neoliberal and neoconservative efforts to shape assumptions concerning valid approaches to inquiry across disciplines (Apple, 2006a, 2006b; Cannella and Lincoln, 2007; Cheek, 2005). Proponents of these conservative political and economic ideologies have attempted to dismiss, if not entirely erase, the contributions of critical scholarship through establishment of a global movement (Denzin, 2009) to narrowly define high-quality, rigorous, and therefore legitimate, educational inquiry. As a result of the escalating influence of conservative ideologies within governmental agencies, higher education institutions, and disciplinary associations such as the American Education Research Association (AERA) and the Association for the Study of Higher Education (ASHE), contemporary higher education scholars are firmly embedded in an era of methodological conservatism (Denzin and Giardina, 2006; Lincoln and Cannella, 2004a, 2004b) defined by organizational practices and principles of inquiry that actively undermine the adoption of critical epistemological and methodological perspectives. For example, the disciplining norms of methodological conservatism are exemplified in the parameters of scientific and evidence-based inquiry articulated in documents such as the NRC's (2002) *Scientific Research in Education,* and market-driven conceptualizations of knowledge production characteristic of the increasingly dominant academic capitalism knowledge/ learning regime (Bok, 2003; Giroux and Giroux, 2004; Slaughter and Leslie, 1997; Slaughter and Rhoades, 2004).

In this chapter we synthesize extant scholarship on the methodological implications stemming from the advancement of a "new scientific orthodoxy" (Howe, 2008) and the rise of academic capitalism as well as explore the significance of these disciplining discourse regimes (Bloch, 2004) for members of historically marginalized communities and higher education scholars seeking to address issues of in/equity within postsecondary institutions.

Critical Qualitative Higher Education Research in the Era of Methodological Conservatism

The Disciplining Regime of Scientifically Based Educational Research

The NRC's (2002) methodological manifesto, *Scientific Research in Education*, marks its tenth anniversary in 2012. The NRC report, co-authored by a committee of sixteen educational scholars charged to "review and synthesize recent literature on the science and practice of scientific educational research and consider how to support high-quality science in a federal education research agency" (NRC, 2002, p. 1), articulates six scientific principles that "underlie all scientific inquiry, including education research" (p. 2):

Scientific Principle 1: Pose significant questions that can be investigated empirically.

Scientific Principle 2: Link research to relevant theory.

Scientific Principle 3: Use methods that permit direct investigation of the questions.

Scientific Principle 4: Provide a coherent and explicit chain of reasoning.

Scientific Principle 5: Replicate and generalize across studies.

Scientific Principle 6: Disclose research to encourage professional scrutiny and critique (NRC, 2002, pp. 3–5).

Although the intentions of the NRC committee were honorable—to chart a "vision for the future of educational research" (NRC, 2002, p. 2)—the product of their deliberations is quite problematic for critical qualitative higher education scholars seeking to address issues of educational in/equity. Of particular concern is Principle 5, which seemingly dismisses epistemological and methodological perspectives that question the utility (or even the possibility) of producing replicable and generalizable research. Scholars who refuse to operate from within the narrow framework of scientific inquiry find their work relegated to the margins of an increasingly conservative academy (Apple, 2006a; Slaughter and Rhoades, 2004), a reality that holds significant implications for both the scholars and the communities they seek to learn from/collaborate with.

For the architects and proponents of the scientific educational research movement (see, for example, Cook, 2002, 2003; Mosteller and Boruch, 2002; Slavin, 2002), the educational policy initiatives of 2001 and 2002[3] were important steps toward narrowly defining the parameters of "legitimate" inquiry, demarcating large-scale, random sample, experimental design studies as the gold standard in educational research. For those educational scholars guided by critical epistemological and methodological perspectives which recognize the political and historically oppressive nature of normative approaches to educational inquiry (Cannella and Lincoln, 2004b; Kincheloe and McLaren, 2005; Potts and Brown, 2005; Strega, 2005), the tenth anniversary of the NRC's (2002) *Scientific Research in Education* is not a cause for celebration but rather a somber event that marks a renewed era of methodological conservatism defined by governmental and institutional attempts to maintain the political, economic, and cultural status quo via control of knowledge production norms, standards, and processes (Bloch, 2004; Cannella and Lincoln, 2004a, 2004b; Denzin, 2009, 2011; Denzin and Giardina, 2006; Lather, 1993, 2004; Lincoln and Cannella, 2004a, 2004b; Lincoln and Tierney, 2004; Schwandt, 2006; St. Pierre, 2004). Unfortunately, although much has been written about the manifestations and implications of methodological conservatism within the broad social science community of qualitative scholars (two issues of *Qualitative Inquiry* were dedicated to the subject in 2004—see Cannella and Lincoln, 2004a; Lincoln and Cannella, 2004a), few researchers have discussed the significance of the science-based research movement for higher education scholarship in particular. We seek to interrupt this silence by initiating dialogue among higher education scholars on the principles and tools of methodological conservatism as well as the implications of these "dangerous discourses" (Lincoln and Cannella, 2004a) for scholars committed to addressing issues of in/equity in postsecondary educational institutions.

Accordingly, in this section our focus is on providing the reader with a synthesis of the scholarly critiques leveled against the science-based educational research movement. In the next chapter we encourage and challenge the reader to move from understanding to action, highlighting several strategies for intervening in the hegemonic practices invoked by the NRC report and similar declarations of methodological conservatism.

It is important to note that the *Reading Excellence Act of 1999*,[4] the *No Child Left Behind Act of 2001,* and the *Education Sciences Reform Act of 2002*—three pieces of legislation commonly referenced when discussing the current federal preference for funding and disseminating science-based educational research—are not isolated acts of U.S. educational policymaking. These legislative initiatives exemplify and are embedded in far-reaching patterns of a "global audit culture" (Denzin, 2009) which seeks to reify neopositivist approaches to the production of knowledge; knowledge which can then be used to inform and justify social policies that sustain existing inequitable power structures (Apple, 2006a, 2006b; Lincoln and Cannella, 2004b). Although the motivations and manifestations of the global audit culture may vary from country to country (Cheek, 2007; Curtis, 2008; Denzin, 2011; Morgan, 2004; St. Pierre, 2004; Torrance, 2008, 2011), the common thread connecting attempts to articulate and enforce national research standards is a "global movement to reassert broadly empiricist and technist approaches to the generation and accumulation of social scientific 'evidence' for policy making" (Torrance, 2011, p. 570). Reductive approaches to the production and assessment of legitimate knowledge include the prioritization of experimental designs within educational research (for example, randomized control trials), increased reliance on quantitative metrics of quality and accountability (for example, use of journal impact factors and citation analysis as proxies for evaluating the significance of a study), adoption of stricter peer review policies, the articulation of guidelines and standards for formatting scientific articles, as well as an escalating preoccupation with definitely determining "what works" with respect to educational practice (Cheek, 2007; Denzin, 2009, 2011; Torrance, 2011).

Examples of the audit culture sweeping across the globe include the U.S. Department of Education's Institute of Education Sciences and What Works

Clearinghouse (Denzin, 2011; St. Pierre, 2004); the Australian Research Quality Framework (Cheek, 2007), the Research Assessment Exercise in the United Kingdom (Broadhead and Howard, 1998; Hare, 2003; Morgan, 2004), and New Zealand's Performance Based Research Fund (Curtis, 2008; Waitere and others, 2011)—initiatives distinct in their evaluation criteria and mechanisms of enforcement but united in a common objective—increased governmental oversight of nationally funded research efforts via the establishment of narrow parameters for recognition of legitimate inquiry (Cheek, 2007; Torrance, 2008, 2011). Within the United States, the global audit culture extends beyond the NRC report and the federal educational research legislation enacted in 2001; it is also embodied in attempts by educational scholars to self-govern the content and quality of scholarship through documents such as the American Educational Research Association's *Definition of Scientifically Based Research* (AERA, 2008), *Standards for Reporting on Empirical Social Science Research in AERA Publications* (AERA, 2006), and *Standards for Reporting on Humanities-Oriented Research in AERA Publications* (AERA, 2009).

Attempts to define and regulate standards for the conduct of rigorous educational inquiry capable of providing credible "evidence" upon which to build rational and cost-effective educational policies have been characterized as a "new scientific orthodoxy" (Howe, 2008), "dangerous discourses" (Lincoln and Cannella, 2004a), and governing "regimes of truth" (Denzin and Giardina, 2006). For critical qualitative scholars, the danger embedded within the scientifically based educational research movement is the perpetuation of the inequitable status quo as a result of conservative attempts to silence innovative methodological perspectives that honor local forms of knowledge and recognize the voices of those who experience discrimination and oppression on a daily basis (Cannella and Lincoln, 2004a, 2004b, 2009). The following excerpt from the AERA *Definition of Scientifically Based Research* (AERA, 2008) offers a prime example of the precise, narrow, and exclusionary language critical qualitative researchers find objectionable in contemporary efforts to describe the nature and aims of educational inquiry:

> *The examination of causal questions requires experimental designs using random assignment or quasi-experimental or other designs*

that substantially reduce plausible competing explanations for the obtained results. These include, but are not limited to, longitudinal designs, case control methods, statistical matching, or time series analyses. This standard applies especially to studies evaluating the impacts of policies and programs on educational outcomes [AERA, 2008, para. 2].

The privileging of "causal questions" remains particularly problematic for critical scholars who resist the unidirectional logic of post/positivism that extends directly from cause-and-effect thinking. Additionally, qualitative methodologists from within and beyond the field of educational research have contested the articulation of universal standards for research quality and rigor on the grounds that documents such as the *Standards for Reporting on Empirical Social Science Research in AERA Publications* and the NRC report produce knowledge hierarchies and disciplining "regimes of truth" (Foucault, 1980) which narrowly define the parameters of legitimate educational inquiry and dismiss as irrelevant those educational scholars who do not subscribe to federally endorsed constructions of scientific research predicated on the principles of objectivity and generalizability (Lincoln, 2005). Given that numerous scholars (Bloch, 2004; Denzin and Giardina, 2006; Lincoln and Cannella, 2004a) have called upon Foucault's notion of "regimes of truth" to explicate the oppressive and punitive function of contemporary discourses on scientifically based educational research, it is important that we elaborate on this argument.

In the essay "Truth and Power," Foucault (1980) calls attention to the power embedded within discursive regimes of truth, "rules of formation of statements which are accepted as scientifically true" (p. 112). Given their power to determine the parameters of truth and acceptable knowledge, discursive regimes such as the NRC Principles of Scientific Inquiry (NRC, 2002) and the *Standards for Reporting on Empirical Social Science Research in AERA Publications* (AERA, 2006)—henceforth referred to as the *Social Science Standards*—act as vehicles of social reproduction, encouraging the development and praise of some knowledge claims and silencing other forms of inquiry considered to be less legitimate (Fraser, 1981). For example, although the architects of the NRC report acknowledge that scientific research "is related to, and often depends on" (NRC, 2002, p. 131) a diverse array of scholarly pursuits, the committee makes a point of distinguishing scientific research in education from "other forms of educational scholarship (e.g., history and philosophy)" and justifies the omission of humanities-based research perspectives from the text given that "they are outside the scope of the committee's charge to focus on scientific research in education" (NRC, 2002, p. 131). AERA also identifies scholarship grounded in the humanities as outside the boundaries of legitimacy defined by the *Social Science Standards*. By explicitly recognizing humanities research as beyond the scope of their charge, the NRC and AERA methodological regulatory committees construct an unambiguous discursive regime of (social) scientific inquiry that excludes research projects informed by theoretical and methodological insights drawn from disciplines such as history, literary theory, philosophy, religion, cultural studies, and the visual arts. Also excluded from consideration as scientific educational research are those studies informed by "extreme epistemological perspectives" (NRC, 2002, p. 25) such as postmodernism, critical race theory, queer theory, and other theoretical perspectives, which question the possibility of producing objective, generalizable knowledge given that all knowledge is mediated by historically constituted and constantly evolving sociological conditions (for example, demographics, geography, culture, economy; Denzin, 2010a; Kincheloe and McLaren, 2005). As alluded to in the introductory pages to this chapter, we view the position of the NRC Report, itself, as emblematic of an "extreme epistemological perspective." It is an extremely positivistic orientation that invokes an overlapping array of regimes of truth for legitimation.

In the interest of acknowledging the rich history and valuable contribution of humanities-oriented educational research, AERA complemented the *Social Science Standards* with *Standards for Reporting on Humanities-Oriented Research in AERA Publications* (AERA, 2009), henceforth referred to as the *Humanities Standards*. While the intent of AERA may have been to expand the sphere of legitimate educational inquiry though the articulation of universal criteria for evaluating the significance, methods, conceptualization, coherence, substantiation, quality of communication, and ethics of educational research conducted outside the carefully demarcated boundaries of the social sciences, these seven *Humanities Standards* ultimately serve to establish yet another disciplining discursive regime that marginalizes critical epistemological and methodological perspectives (Denzin, 2011). Drawing upon disciplinary definitions borrowed from the National Endowment for the Humanities, the AERA *Humanities Standards* focus on "traditional humanities disciplines such as linguistics, literary theory, history, jurisprudence, philosophy, and religion" as well as those educational studies that blur the boundaries between social science and humanities as a result of their theoretical ties to cultural studies, sociology, cultural anthropology, political science and economics (AERA, 2009, pp. 481–482). The *Humanities Standards* only briefly mention, however, the "array of other approaches to studies in education such as critical, arts-based, and narrative" (AERA, 2009, p. 482) inquiry, methods that defy disciplinary affiliation, yet according to AERA, are probably more similar to humanities than social science research and thus are appropriately guided (disciplined) by the *Humanities Standards.*

The implications of including critical methods as an afterthought in the discussion of humanities-oriented educational research are twofold. First, the *Humanities Standards* advance normative criteria for evaluating scholarship that do not acknowledge the distinct epistemological and methodological assumptions of critical inquiry. Standards developed to evaluate the merit and quality of "traditional" humanities research are not well suited for assessing the contribution of critical scholars who view inquiry as a vehicle of collaborative knowledge production, democracy, activism, revolution, and justice (Denzin, 2011; Finley, 2011). Of equal concern is the ease with which the AERA *Social Science* and *Humanities Standards,* as well as the NRC's *Scientific Research in Education,* construct a false dichotomy between humanities and social science research (Howe, 2009), placing contested notions of disciplinary boundaries at the center of contemporary dialogues on the nature of legitimate educational inquiry. Turning scholarly attention to issues of academic discipline and the demarcation of disciplinary methods effectively serves to silence the voices of educational scholars who locate their research across, betwixt, and/or outside disciplinary walls. Within the discursive regime of the AERA *Humanities Standards,* disciplinary orientation (or lack thereof), not epistemological and methodological commitments, is the focus of scrutiny, resulting in the perpetuation of dominant social science and humanities research paradigms that fall far short of realizing the equity and social justice aims of critical qualitative inquiry.

Returning to Foucault's (1980) insight into the disciplining function of discursive regimes, we must recognize the NRC, AERA, and federal government's efforts to articulate and enforce universal principles of scientific inquiry and standards of evidence as exercises of power in the interest of establishing a "monoculture—a single discursive and methodological community that speaks the same language and more important, takes as its concerns the same issues from the same perspectives" (Lincoln and Cannella, 2004b, p. 8). Shrouded in a commonsense rhetoric (Apple, 2006a, 2006b) that extols the noble search for evidence of "what works" in contemporary educational institutions, the monocultural scientific educational research movement actively contributes to the perpetuation of educational inequity via the adoption and enforcement of research norms which silence the voices of scholars and their collaborators (for example, students, parents, teachers, community activists). As such, scholars who seek to initiate educational transformation via the production of local knowledge and community engagement efforts that acknowledge the deep-rooted, complex, and highly contextualized nature of oppression are relegated to the margins of academe (for more on silencing voices of scholars and collaborators in higher education contexts, see Pasque, 2010a). Compounding pressure to adhere to the disciplining discourse of scientific educational research is the escalating influence of the academic capitalism knowledge/learning regime (Slaughter and Rhoades, 2004), a market-driven framework for strengthening the integration of higher education institutions in the new global knowledge economy. In the next section, we shed light on the inextricable relationship between academic capitalism and the methodological conservatism that characterizes contemporary higher education scholarship.

The Methodological Implications of Academic Capitalism

As previously noted, in addition to contesting the methodological regimes of truth embedded in the scientific educational research movement, contemporary qualitative higher education scholars interested in addressing issues of in/equity must also contend with the disciplining norms of *academic capitalism,* a term used to describe the expansion of institutional efforts to secure external revenue via market engagement (for example, the establishment of technology transfer units and other intermediating organizational structures designed to realize the commercial potential of faculty research and instructional resources; Slaughter and Leslie, 1997).[5] Institutions of higher education operate within an academic capitalism knowledge/learning regime (Slaughter and Rhoades, 2004), characterized by adherence to a neoliberal ideology, which views individual economic achievement as a means of advancing the public good. Increasingly, colleges and universities aggressively seek to redraw the boundaries between the public and private sectors, inevitably favoring new boundaries that allow them to participate in a wide variety of entrepreneurial activities and secure additional revenue. Chief among these entrepreneurial efforts are activities focused on marketing the products of academic research (Bok, 2003; Cheek, 2007; Slaughter and Rhoades, 2004; Stein, 2004; Washburn, 2005). Although the strategies, benefits and negative consequences associated with generating revenue via industry–university partnerships, external grants, and technology transfer endeavors have been thoroughly examined within the higher education literature (for example, Bok, 2003; Eckel, Couturier and Luu, 2005; Kirp, 2003; Morphew and Eckel, 2009; Slaughter, 2001; Slaughter and Rhoades, 2004; Stein, 2004; Washburn, 2005), few postsecondary scholars have explored the methodological implications embedded within the academic capitalism knowledge learning regime. Of particular concern in this chapter are the ways in which the expansion of neoliberal ideology and market pressures within the academy contribute to the reproduction of higher education research norms that marginalize innovative critical qualitative perspectives which seek to address issues of educational in/equity via research processes as well as products.

As noted earlier, a defining feature of the academic capitalism knowledge/learning regime (Slaughter and Rhoades, 2004) is adherence to neoliberal principles. Neoliberalism is a political and economic ideology characterized by a belief in the supremacy of the market, a focus on individual economic competition and achievement, and a commitment to reducing state support for social welfare programs and services (Ayers, 2005; Levin, 2007; Slaughter and Rhoades, 2004). Within the neoliberal framework, higher education as a private/individual/economic good is actually considered a public good (for examples, see Bartik, 2005; Brandl and Weber, 1995; Gottlieb and Fogarty, 2003) and the implications of this perspective are far reaching with respect to the development of market-driven norms concerning the nature of faculty work (Etzkowitz, Webster, and Healey, 1998; Powell and Owen-Smith, 2002; Slaughter and Leslie, 1997; Stein, 2004; Washburn, 2005). For example, one strand of academic capitalism scholarship explores the influences of neoliberal ideology and market pressures on knowledge production, contending that faculty speculation about potential profits, *not* the assessment of public benefits, has become the driving force behind the development of faculty research agendas and educational offerings (Eckel, Couturier, and Luu, 2005; Schrecker, 2001, Slaughter, 2001; Slaughter and Leslie, 1997). These scholars worry that faculty members have forsaken public interest research in favor of chasing elusive commercial ventures that offer the promise of institutional prestige and individual profit.

Although the context and nature of educational research are quite distinct from those academic disciplines often understood as directly aligned with the market (that is, biotechnology, pharmacology, computer science), higher educational scholars are not immune to the rising influence of neoliberalism (Apple, 2006a) and are therefore also susceptible to the pressures of engaging in market-oriented research. Cheek (2005) elaborates on several of the new neoliberal norms faculty must contend with when research is framed as a market activity:

> *It is the market, not necessarily peers, that determine the worth of research, and even what research will be done. Furthermore, this marketplace is tightly regulated in terms of the means of obtaining funding, what actually is funded, the way research performance is assessed, and the reporting that researchers must do both about their research and the way that they use their time in general [p. 405].*

Within the contemporary academic capitalism knowledge/learning regime, the market-driven push to secure funding and publish has translated into rushed, atheoretical scholarship which makes limited contribution in terms of knowledge production, and more importantly, social transformation (Cheek, 2005). In short, such texts simply seek to describe and/or predict manifestations of the status quo; they do not seek to intervene within and critically alter the myriad social processes that reproduce patterns of educational inequity, discrimination, and injustice.

Similar to the disciplining regimes of truth embedded within the scientifically based educational research movement, the policies and practices associated with academic capitalism (for example, market-driven promotion and tenure guidelines, funding policies, peer review norms, and accountability metrics) serve to constrain and marginalize the work of critical qualitative higher education scholars seeking to address issues of in/equity via innovative and empowering research designs (Cannella and Lincoln, 2007; Greenwood and Levin, 2000). Scholars who contest, rather than advance, a neoliberal educational agenda of market supremacy are not likely to receive the funding and recognition essential for survival in the academic capitalism knowledge/learning regime that characterizes modern colleges and universities. This perspective is evident in Brandl and Weber's (1995) projection for the state of Minnesota that the "weakest" faculty research agendas and institutions will not survive the "post-secondary marketplace" (p. 25).

A prime example of the often unexamined methodological implications embedded within the expansion of academic capitalism is the recent proliferation of calls for mixed methods research by scholars and funding agencies who tout the scholarly merits (including fiscal efficiency) of combining quantitative and qualitative approaches to the study of social phenomena (Creswell, 2011a; Creswell, Carroll Klassen, Plano Clark, and Clegg Smith, 2011; Griffin and Museus, 2011; Johnson and Onwuegbuzie, 2004; Teddlie and Tashakkori, 2011). The increasing dominance of mixed methods research within the discursive regime of federal funding guidelines and opportunities is exemplified in the recent National Institutes of Health report (Creswell, Carroll Klassen, Plano Clark, and Clegg Smith, 2011), *Best Practices for Mixed Methods Research in the Health Sciences,* which offers both prospective NIH research funding applicants and proposal reviewers guidance in the development and identification of rigorous, high-quality research designs capable of effectively addressing the nation's most pressing health problems. Given that health research is the second largest research and development budget function of the federal government (behind national defense of course; Bennoff, 2010), the formal articulation of mixed methods research as a NIH funding priority serves as compelling motivation for scholars both within and beyond the health disciplines to develop research proposals that embrace mixed method designs.

As pressure to engage in funded research intensifies within Colleges of Education, critical higher education scholars are increasingly called upon to pursue and design research projects that forsake their epistemological and methodological commitments and, more importantly, the interests of historically marginalized communities, in an effort to demonstrate alignment with the goals and preferred methodological frameworks of funding agencies (Cheek, 2005; Giddings, 2006). Indeed, Cheek (2005) provides an insightful discussion of the tensions qualitative researchers must navigate when engaged in the "practice and politics of funded qualitative research," raising a series of questions qualitative scholars should ask themselves prior to drafting and/or contributing to funding proposals. A few of Cheek's questions are paraphrased below:

- Is it better to critique the system from within as a funded qualitative researcher or does securing funding equate with "selling out" and perpetuating the status quo?
- What are the implications of accepting invitations to "add a bit of qualitative research" to a larger grant-funded project? Is the qualitative component of the study viewed as an "add on" or an integral part of the study?
- Am I conducting research that matters or research that can generate funding?

While there are no right or wrong answers to Cheek's queries, we appreciate her call to wrestle with substantive issues of purpose, epistemology, and methodology when engaging in funded qualitative research, as these matters are ignored often within the discourse of academic capitalism and dismissed as irrelevant by the proponents of a pragmatist research paradigm that valorizes mixed methods research devoid of epistemological and methodological roots (Lincoln, 2010).

Characterizing mixed methods research as positivism dressed in drag, Giddings (2006) presents a cogent and cautionary analysis of the (un)intended consequences that lie ahead if the assumptions, principles, and practices of mixed methods, which offer "cover for the continuing hegemony of positivism, and maintain the marginalisation of non-positivist research" (p. 195), are not challenged by critical qualitative scholars who value local knowledge, activism, and equity above revenue generation and fiscal efficiency. Similar to the disciplining discursive regimes of the AERA *Humanities* and *Social Science Standards* (AERA, 2009 and 2006, respectively) and the NRC's (2002) *Scientific Research in Education*, contemporary research funding protocols such as the NIH's *Best Practices for Mixed Methods Research in the Health Sciences* (Creswell, Carroll Klassen, Plano Clark, and Clegg Smith, 2011), turn the researcher's attention away from the possibility of challenging dominant (oppressive) epistemological and methodological perspectives and instead require they tend to technical matters of method in the interest of securing the funding necessary to retain their professional positions within the academy. While the favoritism currently displayed by funding agencies for mixed methods research may be a passing fad, it is emblematic of the methodological tensions embedded within the academic capitalism knowledge/learning regime—tensions that challenge critical qualitative scholars to reconcile their commitment to engaging in transformative educational research with institutional expectations for revenue generation.

The continued dismissal of critical qualitative methodological perspectives as a result of the scientifically based research movement and simultaneous rise of academic capitalism knowledge/learning regime holds real and dangerous consequences for both scholars of higher education as well as the historically marginalized communities that serve as the focus of their research and activism. In the following section we review these consequences in more depth, taking up a guiding question of this monograph: What is at stake if dominant methodological perspectives continue to frame the principles and practices of higher education inquiry?

What Is at Stake in the Era of Methodological Conservatism?

Implications for Historically Marginalized Communities
The increasing dominance of the scientific research and academic capitalism discourse regimes within the higher education scholarly community holds

powerful implications for individuals located within and beyond university boundaries. Of particular concern are the consequences of methodological conservatism for individuals and communities who regularly encounter individual, institutional, and/or societal discrimination and oppression. Critical qualitative scholars strive to work with and for historically marginalized communities in the pursuit of social justice and educational equity (and, at times, are a part of said communities). The relegation of their work to the academic hinterlands and the perpetuation of the methodological status quo have significant material consequences for students and their families struggling to gain and maintain equitable access to postsecondary education. Specifically, the preservation of discriminatory educational practices, policies, and environments impacts who our educational institutions are driven to serve. As such, the very design of educational programs, opportunities to develop social and cultural capital, and the ability to develop a sense of agency amidst an increasingly structured educational environment may reify or disrupt sociopolitical, economic, and historical norms. Maintaining the status quo continues the subjugation of the unique histories, beliefs, and knowledge bases that shape individual and collective identities within culturally diverse communities. Simply put, critical scholars cannot allow this trend to continue.

As noted earlier, what is particularly pernicious about the discourses of scientific educational research and academic capitalism is the cloaking of these conservative agendas within a commonsense rhetoric intended to solicit the support of the very communities these movements work to disempower (Apple, 2006a). In recent history, architects of neoliberal and neoconservative educational policy have strategically employed progressive, provocative, and "plain speaking" language (for example, No Child Left Behind, What Works, evidence-based inquiry, data-driven reform; Apple, 2006a, p. 83) in the interest of capturing the attention, imagination, and, in some cases, the votes, of citizens (the exclusionary reference to citizens here is intentional as a large contingent of conservative policy makers have actively worked to diminish the social, educational, and economic rights afforded undocumented immigrants). For example, Ward Connerly's American Civil Rights Institute, a "national civil rights organization created to educate the public on the harms of racial and gender preferences" (American Civil Rights Institute, n.d., para. 1) and a prominent player in the movement to repeal or block higher education affirmative action programs via state ballot initiatives, is a prime example of the Right's powerful, strategic and manipulative use of progressive language (that is, civil rights) to garner popular support for an organization that seeks to dismantle educational and government policies intended to promote educational equity within historically marginalized communities. Apple (2006a) eloquently elaborates on the hidden meanings and agendas often embedded within neoliberal discourses such as academic capitalism, highlighting the seductive, yet ultimately disempowering, logic of the market:

> *Neoliberals argue that making the market the ultimate arbiter of social worthiness will eliminate politics and its accompanying irrationality from our educational and social decisions. Efficiency and cost-benefit analysis will be the engines of social and educational transformation. Yet among the ultimate effects of such "economizing" and "depoliticizing" strategies is actually to make it even harder to interrupt the growing inequalities in resources and power that so deeply characterize this society. . . . This very politicization makes it very difficult for the needs of those with less economic, political, and cultural power to be accurately heard and acted on in ways that deal with the true depth of the problem [pp. 36–37].*

Although Apple does not explicitly address the methodological implications embedded within neoliberal approaches to educational reform, his assertion that the adoption of market-driven accountability measures (for example, efficiency, cost-benefit analyses) undermines the potential for historically marginalized communities to substantively inform or participate in the educational policy development and processes calls attention to the far-reaching effects of methodological conservatism.

The escalating dominance of mixed methods educational research is yet another example of neoliberal discourse that relies on inherently appealing and progressive rhetoric to advance a conservative and exclusionary research agenda (Giddings, 2006) that has material consequences for historically marginalized populations. For example, Teddlie and Tashakkoi (2011) talk of pragmatism, methodological eclecticism, paradigm pluralism, celebration of diversity at all levels of the research enterprise, and a tendency toward balance and compromise in their description of mixed methods research. This methodological phrasing is difficult to challenge given its seemingly enlightened tone; however, Giddings (2006) warns that on an ideological level, mixed methods research often "continues the privileging and dominance of the positivist scientific tradition" (p. 202), dismissing as inefficient (or, worse, illegitimate) those research endeavors which eschew the generalizability aims of the scientific method in favor of collaborative, contextualized inquiry that fosters material change in the daily lives of research participants/collaborators.

Critical higher education scholars who view research as a vehicle of resistance, empowerment and transformation place the voices and experiences of the historically marginalized at the center of inquiry, studying *with* rather than conducting research *on* those who experience discrimination and oppression on a daily basis (Dillard, 2000; Fine, 1994; Gildersleeve, 2010; Jackson and Mazzei, 2009; Pasque, 2010b; Smith, 1999; Wilson and Yellow Bird, 2005). These scholars question the utility and/or possibility of promoting social change via government-endorsed scientific research designs that fail to acknowledge the complex, historically mediated nature of educational inequities. Although critical qualitative higher education scholars can and do engage in meaningful inquiry beyond the reach of the methodological conservative movement (Abes and Kasch, 2007; Brayboy, 2004; Gildersleeve, 2010; McLaughlin and Tierney, 1993; Solórzano and Yosso, 2001; Stewart, 2008; Wagner, 2011; Winkle-Wagner, 2009; Wong, 2011; Yakaboski, 2011), the escalating influence of the scientific and academic capitalism discourses pushes this scholarship to the margins of the academy and policy development arenas, undermining, as Apple (2006a) alludes to, the potential for these critical works to substantively inform and shape higher education policy (Howe, 2009; Johnson, 2008; Lincoln, 2005; St. Pierre, 2004). Thus, there is a great deal at stake for members of historically marginalized communities when the epistemological and methodological perspectives that honor the complexity of (historical and contemporary) lived experiences are explicitly rejected from consideration as legitimate forms of inquiry—it is the perpetuation of a status quo as characterized by educational stratification, economic disparity, and diminished opportunity.

Although we now turn our attention to the implications of methodological conservatism for critical higher education scholars, more specifically the tensions these researches encounter in their endeavor to address issues of educational in/equity while simultaneously navigating/resisting the disciplining discourse regimes of science-based educational research and academic capitalism, it is important to note the overlap between the consequences these regimes of truth hold for scholars and members of historically marginalized communities. The failure of critical higher education scholars to productively negotiate methodological regimes of truth does indeed hold significant, material implications for individuals located beyond the academy, as the transformative potential of research processes and products is fundamentally a matter of researcher ethics and actions. Although we opted to separate the implications discussion into two discrete sections for organizational clarity, we view these conversations as overlapping and inextricably connected.

Implications for Critical Qualitative Higher Education Scholars
The growing dominance of the scientifically based educational research and academic capitalism discourse regimes also hold significant consequences for higher education scholars seeking to contest the status quo and promote positive social change via their research and community engagement efforts. Critical qualitative higher education scholars guided by what the architects of methodological conservatism deem "extreme epistemological perspectives" (NRC, 2002) are subject to professional censure and scholarly punishments (e.g., increased scrutiny by institutional review boards, diminished funding and publication opportunities) that undercut the norms of academic freedom and job security historically associated with tenure track and tenured faculty positions (Bloch, 2004; Cannella and Lincoln, 2004a; Cheek, 2007; Lincoln, 2005; Lincoln and Cannella, 2004a; Lincoln and Tierney, 2004; Strega, 2005; Tierney and Corwin, 2007).

In this section we synthesize the methodological literature within and beyond the field of higher education that discusses what is at stake for critical qualitative scholars who choose to disrupt, interrogate, and challenge the disciplining regimes of truth that characterize methodologically conservative promotion and tenure standards, funding and publication peer review processes, as well as human subjects research approval. Our aim in shedding light on the material consequences associated with engaging in what Cannella and Lincoln (2004b) describe as critical social science—research that seeks to realize the "liberatory possibilities" of inquiry (p. 301)—is not to discourage critical higher education scholars from engaging in transformative scholarship, but rather to raise awareness of the consequences that may stem from enacting critical methodological commitments in the hopes of better preparing critical scholars to productively navigate and overcome professional roadblocks.

A common thread connecting methodological reflections on the professional consequences of engaging in critical qualitative scholarship is an awareness that the critical scholar's work (including research, teaching, and community engagement efforts) is subject to evaluation processes and standards governed by a dominant ideology that does not value, or in extreme cases does not recognize, the norms and commitments of critical inquiry. In the contemporary era of methodological conservatism, the dominant ideologies shaping promotion and tenure decisions, publication standards, and funding mechanisms are the disciplining discourses of scientifically based educational research and academic capitalism. Although the longstanding scholarly norm of academic freedom theoretically provides critical higher education scholars the professional protection necessary to pursue politically charged and methodologically innovative research projects focused on identifying and ameliorating conditions of educational inequity, the regimes of truth that define the modern era of methodological conservatism have significantly eroded the intellectual freedom historically afforded tenure and tenure track faculty (Lincoln, 2005; Lincoln and Tierney, 2004; Tierney and Corwin, 2007).

One arena in which critical qualitative scholars commonly find themselves forced to navigate threats to their academic freedom is the campus approval process for engaging in human subjects research. In accordance with the Common Rule, a set of federal regulations codified in 1991 that govern human subject research, higher education scholars seeking to study (with) humans must seek approval of their research design from a panel of peer reviewers deemed by their institution as "sufficiently qualified through the experience and expertise . . . to ascertain the acceptability of proposed research in terms of institutional commitments and regulations, applicable law, and standards of professional conduct and practice" (Common Rule, 1991). A number of critical qualitative scholars both within and beyond higher education (Koro-Ljungberg, Gemignani, Brodeur, and Kmiec, 2007; Lincoln, 2005; Lincoln and Tierney, 2004; Nelson, 2004; Tierney and Corwin, 2007) have called attention to the disciplining function of institutional review board (IRB) processes, expressing particular frustration that research informed by non-dominant epistemological and innovative methodological perspectives is subject to review for compliance with the Common Rule's narrow definition of research as "a systematic investigation, including research development, testing and evaluation, designed to develop or contribute to generalizable knowledge" (Common Rule, 1991). Firmly anchored in the epistemological and methodological assumptions of positivism, IRB applications demand critical higher education scholars conform to the principles of scientific inquiry by completing standard application protocols which reproduce the rigid norms and structures of the medical research model (Koro-Ljungberg, Gemignani, Brodeur, and Kmiec, 2007). Failure to submit IRB applications that comply with the Common Rule's narrow framework of legitimate inquiry will likely result in one or more requests from IRB to revise the application, requiring the researchers to spend valuable time justifying their professional competencies and/or the appropriateness of their innovative research designs (Lincoln and Tierney, 2004; Tierney and Corwin, 2007). For example, inherent in Participatory Action Research is a commitment to collaboratively developing research designs with participants (including identification of the problem/s and research questions) with the assumption that "ordinary people can understand and change their own lives through research" (Brydon-Miller and others, 2011, p. 388). Failure to provide a precise research design prior to conversations with participants, however, is cause for concern for many IRBs.

Perhaps even more problematic than delaying the start of a research project as a result of a prolonged IRB approval process is the pressure placed upon the scholar to compromise the integrity of the original research design by adopting language and practices incongruent with the scholar's non-dominant methodological perspectives (for example, requiring the researcher to develop a formal interview protocol rather than recognizing the scholar's ability to exercise professional judgment in the development of relevant and sensitive questions as they emerge during the course of an unstructured interview; Koro-Ljungberg, Gemignani, Brodeur, and Kmiec, 2007; Tierney and Corwin, 2007). Lincoln and Tierney (2004) provide a compelling explanation of what is at stake for contemporary critical qualitative higher education scholars subject to the disciplining regime of truth embedded in IRB approval processes:

> *Failure to obtain permission to conduct qualitative studies or mandates that such studies be conducted in positivist fashion will greatly undermine educational researchers' ability to uncover hidden aspects of social arrangements that contribute to unequal schooling, lower persistence rates of minority college students, who other less transparent educational processes [p. 224].*

Koro-Ljungberg, Gemignani, Brodeur, and Kmiec (2007) echo Lincoln and Tierney's (2004) concern regarding the constraints on academic freedom and methodological pluralism imposed by IRB processes and extend the argument by suggesting a connection between the regulatory rule of the IRB and evaluations of a research project's funding potential. Specifically, Koro-Ljungberg and her co-authors assert that the IRB's formal authority to determine the legitimacy of research not only influences researcher behavior in the form of research designs which conform to the scientific principles of the Common Rule, but also shape the behavior of potential funding agents who are unlikely to fund research initiatives that fail to comply with the dominant inquiry paradigm endorsed by IRBs. Cognizant of the increasing role external funding plays in recruitment, tenure, and promotion decisions, critical higher education scholars are frequently forced to choose between engaging in methodologically innovative, transformative research that is unlikely to secure significant external funding or maximizing their funding potential through the pursuit of research projects that abide by dominant norms of inquiry approved by the National Research Council, IRBs, and other advocates of scientifically based educational research.

Although we recognize critical higher education scholars can and do choose to occupy many positions along the spectrum of funded research and the acquisition of external funding does not necessarily undermine the transformative potential of inquiry, the escalating influence of the academic capitalism regime of truth necessitates that critical scholars carefully reflect on the implications, for both themselves and historically marginalized communities, embedded in the pursuit and acceptance of external research funding. Indeed, Cheek (2005) asserts, "funding itself is not the problem—funding is useful as an enabler of qualitative research. Problems arise if funding becomes the end, rather than the means, and qualitative research (or a variant thereof) is subverted to the expedient end of gaining that funding" (p. 408). Of particular concern to Cheek is the potential for the funding pressure associated with academic capitalism to foster a shift in faculty identities from scholar to entrepreneur which will in turn bring about substantive changes in the daily practices and norms of academic life as well as fundamentally alter faculty research agendas. For example, confronted with need to increase extramural funding in order to receive favorable promotion and tenure evaluations, entrepreneurial qualitative scholars may opt to engage in research likely to be deemed fundable as a result of adherence to the principles and norms of methodological conservatism, rather than designing research that places the needs and interests of historically marginalized communities at the center of inquiry (Cheek, 2005; Greenwood and Levin, 2000; Koro-Ljungberg, Gemignani, Brodeur, and Kmiec, 2007).

A third venue in which critical qualitative higher education scholars must learn to confront and navigate the disciplining discourse regimes of methodological conservatism is the process of academic publishing. Numerous critical qualitative scholars (Cheek, 2007; Denzin, 2009; Greenwood and Levin, 2000; Stanley, 2007; Torrance, 2008, 2011) have reflected on the ways in which normative statements regarding the acceptable format and content of educational research articles (for example, AERA, 2006), the proliferation of quantitative metrics for evaluating journal quality coupled with escalating pressure for faculty to publish in "top-tier" journals, and the disciplining norms of peer review serve to privilege the perpetuation of dominant knowledge regimes that uphold the political and economic status quo, preserve educational inequity, and undermine the diversity of scholars and scholarly perspectives in the academy.

Stanley (2007) offers a compelling description of the disciplining features and dangerous consequences embedded in journal editorial review processes, focusing in particular on the role of journal editors and reviewers in sustaining master narratives:

> *A master narrative is a script that specifies and controls how some social processes are carried out. Furthermore, there is a master narrative operating in academia that often defines and limits what is valued as scholarship and who is entitled to create scholarship. This is problematic, because the dominant group in academia writes most research and, more often than not, they are White men. Members of marginalized groups, such as women and people of color, have had little or no input into the shaping of this master narrative. Therefore, research on marginalized groups by members of marginalized groups that reveals experiences that counter master narratives is often compared against the White norm [p. 14].*

Stanley argues that the dominance of the white male perspective on journal editorial review boards (as exhibited in the racial and gender composition of these boards as well as in the adoption of review standards predicated on the knowledge production norms articulated by senior scholars—also likely to be white men) serves to silence counternarratives that draw upon diverse epistemological and methodological perspectives in the interest of interrupting the hegemonic status quo. Unable to secure favorable reviews of their scholarship from mainstream educational research journals given their rejection of claims to objectivity, generalizable knowledge, and color-blind scholarship (Alemán, Salazar, Rorrer, and Parker, 2011), critical qualitative scholars struggle to meet numerical and journal quality expectations outlined in tenure and promotion protocols, and thus run the risk of the institution terminating their academic appointment.

Similar to the discussion of constraints imposed by the disciplining discourses of IRBs, although the norm of academic freedom theoretically protects the right of critical qualitative researchers to engage in work they deem of scholarly significance, within the daily reality of methodological conservatism, escalating expectations to publish in top-tier, mainstream educational research journals fundamentally limit the intellectual autonomy of critical qualitative higher education scholars (Cheek, 2007). As a result, knowledge production within the field of higher education is likely to remain firmly anchored in the dominant epistemological and methodological norms of those in power, the economic and political elite who stand to benefit the most from maintaining the inequitable status quo (Greenwood and Levin, 2000). We are reminded of critical discourse analyst Norman Fairclough (2001) who asks that we interrogate "whether those who benefit most from the way social life is now organized have an interest in the problem not being resolved" (p. 236), or in some cases, remaining oblivious to the problem completely.

As illustrated in the preceding discussion of the manifestations and consequences of methodological conservatism within IRB applications, research funding expectations, and academic publishing norms, a great deal is at stake for critical higher education scholars who decide to adopt innovative methodological perspectives such as those mentioned in the previous chapter. Bloch (2004) offers additional insight on the professional punishments encountered by researchers who opt to resist the disciplining discourse regimes of academic capitalism and scientifically based educational research:

> *This governing of those who are abnormal in the conduct of research—or the understanding of rigor—or the interpretation or use of science—creates a disciplinary margin. Researchers who choose other ways of knowing, looking, or reflecting critically on knowledge construction, selection, and reproduction are positioned as in this margin. Although the margin is not a bad place to be, this particular circumstance creates a group of scholars who are always identified as less legitimate, and/or oppositional, and not as fully accepting of the norms of good science as others who, in fact become established as abnormal in the real science of research in education [p. 102].*

Although some critical scholars may relish their status as academic outlaws or activists, banishment to the academy's margins for failing to adhere to the principles and procedures of scientific educational research or the market-driven priorities of academic capitalism is particularly problematic for emerging critical higher education scholars who may have a difficult time accumulating the publication and funding record needed to secure a faculty position and survive the tenure review. This process continues as associate professors seek full professor positions, yet may not have secured substantial external grant funding in order to be seriously considered at the level of full professor. To be sure, it is possible to conduct transformative educational research if one is employed outside institutions of higher education (for example, researchers and policy analysts may be found on staff rosters of nonprofit organizations, think tanks, consulting firms, and government agencies); however, the forced or voluntary retreat of critical scholars to off-campus research positions will only serve to reify master narratives and norms of methodological conservatism within the academy, ultimately contributing to the continued production of research that fails to examine and address the complex conditions of educational in/equity in higher education. We must also acknowledge that organizations outside institutions of higher education have similar issues of marketization and capitalism to contend with on a regular basis.

The aim of this chapter was to explicate the macro- and mezzo-level influences that mediate the micro (daily) practices of critical qualitative higher education inquiry. Specifically, we explored the numerous tensions encountered by critical higher education scholars situated within institutions and disciplinary organizations increasingly dominated by neoliberal ideology. Over the course of the past decade, the macro-level influence of neoliberalism has been translated into an ever-increasing number of disciplining discursive regimes (intervening at the mezzo level) which seek to narrowly define high-quality, rigorous, and therefore legitimate, educational inquiry. These discursive regimes, exemplified in texts such as *Scientific Research in Education* (NRC, 2002), *Standards for Reporting on Empirical Social Science Research in AERA Publications* (AERA, 2006), *Standards for Reporting on Humanities-Oriented Research in AERA Publications* (AERA, 2009), as well as protocols for securing federal research funding and institutional IRB approval, seek to govern the aims, nature, and outcomes of educational research by specifying behavioral norms and valid methods and simultaneously turning attention away from the more ideologically contested issues of epistemology and methodology. The contemporary preoccupation with the identification of sound research technique (randomized control trial, mixed method, representation of evidence) and disciplinary affiliation (social sciences versus humanities) intentionally ignores those educational scholars who wish to challenge the very epistemological and methodological foundations on which the discursive regimes of scientific inquiry and academic capitalism are constructed.

As discussed at length in this chapter, the ideological and material manifestations of methodological conservatism hold significant and dangerous consequences for both critical qualitative higher education scholars and the historically marginalized individuals with whom they work. Specifically, the discursive regimes which currently govern conceptualizations of legitimate and productive educational inquiry serve to perpetuate the inequitable and oppressive status quo by dismissing as illegitimate the efforts of scholars and their community collaborators to engage in research as a form of resistance and social change. Fortunately, we do not believe that all hope for addressing critical concerns regarding social justice and educational in/equity in higher education has vanished in the contemporary era of methodological conservatism (recall our adherence to a Foucaultian hyperpessimistic activism offered in the first chapter of this monograph). In the final chapter, we explore opportunities and strategies for resisting methodological conservatism from within the academy, articulating a call to action for both emerging and senior qualitative higher education scholars.

Opportunities for Resisting Methodological Conservatism: A Call to Action

W̲E HAVE ARGUED THROUGHOUT this monograph that critical qualitative methodological approaches in higher education should be congruent with epistemological perspectives and include research processes reflective of educational equity toward social justice. We argue that dominant traditions of qualitative inquiry fail to address the fundamental philosophical underpinnings of in/equity in higher education. Given the significant consequences of the methodological conservative movement for both critical higher education scholars and the marginalized communities they/we seek to work with (and, at times, are a part of), it is imperative that researchers committed to non-dominant epistemological and methodological perspectives disrupt the disciplining discourse regimes of academic capitalism and scientifically based educational research.

In this final chapter, we issue a *call to action through intervention* as we draw on extant qualitative methodology scholarship to describe numerous opportunities and strategies for confronting the oppressive knowledge systems that undermine the equity aims of critical qualitative higher education research. As such (and to reiterate), this monograph is not directed toward scholars and practitioners seeking general discussions of qualitative methods, but instead focuses on more in-depth discussions of critical qualitative inquiry and implications for the field and communities un/touched by the field. We offer this final chapter as an intentional invitation for reflection, dialogue, contestation, and action in higher education research. Specifically, we highlight the transformative potential embedded in researcher reflexivity activities, efforts to engage within the academy to challenge dominant paradigms of methodological conservatism and support critical qualitative researchers, new approaches to socializing emerging scholars to the roles and responsibilities of academe, and the cultivation of the abilities associated with speaking to and collaborating with multiple constituencies within and beyond the academy.

Although the work of intervention is daunting and exhausting, it is also necessary. Indeed, we follow Cameron McCarthy, who asserts, "We must think possibility within constraint; that is the condition of our time" (as cited in Apple, 2006b, p. 28). The preceding chapters acknowledged the ideological and material constraints imposed on critical qualitative scholars, but now it is time we turn our attention to the promise of possibility and transformation through intervention.

Reflexivity as Intervention

Reflexivity and self-knowledge are fundamental elements of qualitative research and are of particular importance in the process of critical inquiry (Chaudhry, 2000; Gibbs, Costley, Armsby and Trakakis, 2007; Gilgun, 2008, 2010; Jones, Torres, and Arminio, 2006; Lather, 2003; Milner, 2007; Richardson and St. Pierre, 2005; Rossman and Rallis, 2003; Salzman, 2002). On a number of occasions, we have heard and received challenges from critical qualitative scholars who bemoan the amount of attention qualitative scholars direct toward themselves, "navel gazing" at the expense of focusing on the exploitation and discrimination of marginalized individuals, groups, and communities. Rather than portraying research as a zero sum game with reflexive efforts regarded as time away from fostering social change, critical higher education scholars need to recognize reflexivity and self-awareness as interventions in methodological conservatism and opportunities for advancing the equity aims of critical scholarship.

Earlier, we argued that epistemology, ontology, and axiology undergird approaches to research—albeit in a visible or invisible manner, each with varying implications. In addition, researchers who explore the complexities of self—values, goals, ambitions, interests, strengths and limitations—in relation to their past experiences within historical, sociopolitical, economic, and intercultural contexts—are more likely to develop the self-sovereignty needed to resist the seductions and pressures of academic capitalism and the scientifically based educational research movement. In other words, researchers participate with a discerning eye and engaging voice of change toward educational equity.

Reflection is both an easy and difficult proposition. Theoretically it is easy to rationalize the need for reflection and understand how it informs research. Practically, however, reflection is a much more nuanced and complex endeavor. Bobbi Harro offers the cycles of socialization (2000b) and liberation (2000a) which may serve as touchstones for researchers to explore self and agency. The cycle of socialization process within a culture is "*pervasive* (coming from all sides and sources), *consistent* (patterned and predictable), *circular* (self-supporting), *self-perpetuating* (intradependent) and often *invisible* (unconscious and unmanned)" (Harro, 2000b, p. 15). As such, dominant perspectives are reinforced through institutional and cultural messages that result in dissonance, silence, collusion, ignorance, violence, and internalized patterns of power. Researchers have choices to reflect on their own socialization process and do nothing—and thereby perpetuate the status quo—or make change by raising consciousness, interrupting patterns, educating one's self and others, and taking action in various manners. Later in this chapter, we provide options for intervention and change by critical qualitative researchers in the academy.

Harro's (2000a) cycle of liberation regarding individual, collaborative, community, and culture change requires:

> *a struggle against discrimination based on race, class, gender, sexual identity, ableism and age—those barriers that keep large portions of the population from having access to economic and social justice, from being able to participate fully in the decisions affecting our lives, from having a full share of both the rights and responsibilities of living in a free society [p. 450].*

Such liberatory and emancipatory perspectives in a research context may interrupt dominant paradigms of oppression through critical qualitative inquiry and transformational and collaborative relationships. As mentioned in "Confronting Qualitative Inquiry in Higher Education" and "Critical Concerns for Qualitative Inquiry in Higher Education," reflection on epistemological perspectives matter and the critical turn calls forth an emphasis on daily liberatory practices within localized material—and more macro-oriented discursive—contexts even as it foregrounds axiological questions of ethics and values of systematic change.

Reflective questions posed by Cannella and Lincoln (2004b) and Cheek (2005, 2007) speak directly to the challenges of conducting critical qualitative research in the modern era and provide a means for scholars to translate enhanced self-awareness into productive action. For example, Cannella and Lincoln (2004b) ask scholars committed to advancing critical social science to take up the following epistemological and methodological questions, "How is resistance to research placed at the center? How do we continually contest our research practices while at the same time continuing to conduct research? and How can we question 'knowing' itself as a purpose of research? Are there other questions that we should be asking rather than 'What do we know (or experience)?'" (p. 305). As such, a researcher is reflexively critical of that in which s/z/he is actively engaged.

In a similar, although slightly more pragmatic vein, Cheek (2005, 2007) asks qualitative researchers to critically reflect on the role funding plays in the determination of research agendas, posing questions intended to help scholars recognize and resist the rising influence of academic capitalism. Building on her own responses to questions such as, "What are the implications of accepting invitations to 'add a bit of qualitative research' to a larger grant-funded project?" (2005, p. 389), Cheek translates enhanced reflexivity into tangible strategies for productively and ethically navigating pressures to secure ever increasing amounts of extramural research funding. Specifically, she encourages qualitative scholars to intentionally negotiate with funding agencies the terms of data ownership, dissemination of findings, participant confidentiality, and expectations regarding the nature of project deliverables (for example, the number, format, and content of reports the researcher must provide the funder). Cheek's concrete strategies for confronting the disciplining discourse regime of academic capitalism underscore the importance of reflexivity as a tool of resistance—those who have a strong sense of self are likely to be more comfortable and confident in advocating for the interests of the marginalized communities that serve as the focus of their research and community engagement efforts. In addition, they/we will be more comfortable and confident in advocating for change within the very structures that confine, discriminate, oppress, and/or perpetuate the status quo.

Further, we encourage faculty to incorporate such reflective questioning into qualitative research classes at both introductory and advanced levels, as we expand on later in this chapter. In a discussion of writing as a means of scholarly self-discovery, Colyar (2006) suggests reflective writing discussions be included in qualitative methodology courses. This practice would give importance to the role of reflexivity in higher education research and simultaneously hold individual researchers accountable for their reflective practices. The emphasis here is on writing as a process that assists researchers in understanding the research and themselves—not on writing as a product, which is a pitfall for many scholars. To be sure, in order to socialize graduate students on the importance of reflexivity, instructors must first acknowledge their own reflexive perspectives on self, participants, social identities, funding, what and how we know, congruence throughout the research process, cycles of socialization and liberation, manifestations of power, and myriad issues.

Institutional and Organizational Intervention

Scholarly reflections on possible opportunities for confronting and resisting methodological conservatism have also focused on interventions at the level of specific campuses and academic organizations (for example, professional associations, journal editorial review boards) where the relationship between faculty and institution is multidirectional. For example, rather than merely lamenting the continued marginalization of critical qualitative scholarship by IRB boards, numerous educational researchers have called on critical scholars to seek change from within the human subjects review process by volunteering to serve as members and even chairs of review boards (Cannella, 2004; Koro-Ljungberg, Gemignani, Brodeur, and Kmiec, 2007; Lincoln, 2005; Lincoln and Cannella, 2004b; Tierney and Lincoln, 2004). Participating in the IRB process as a reviewer affords critical qualitative education scholars the opportunity to understand and counter the objections raised by peers when evaluating the merits and appropriateness of research designs informed by nondominant epistemological and methodological perspectives. Additionally, as an IRB insider, scholars may have an opportunity to organize IRB training and continuing education opportunities that expand the review panel's awareness of and appreciation for innovative approaches to social science inquiry (Lincoln, 2005).

Additional examples of intervention through institutional resistance and activism within the academy include serving as a member of a department's promotion and tenure committee, chairing faculty search committees, volunteering on a campus research award review panel, and taking the time to nominate critical qualitative colleagues and students for scholarly awards (Lincoln and Cannella, 2004b). Importantly, "intervening" means that critical scholars do more than simply serve in these capacities, but also voice complicating perspectives and shape decisions. Kezar, Gallant, and Lester (2011) found that hiring like-minded social activists was an effective tactic for promoting institutional transformation, highlighting the importance of faculty search committee participation. Further, Chesler, Lewis, and Crowfoot (2005) expand on intentional strategies for organizational change in academic settings that tend to both incremental and radical goals for change in the face of opposition, specifically in the face of racism. To be sure, these acts are time-consuming but they also raise the profile of critical qualitative work on campus, initiating dialogue among committee members concerning the legitimacy of innovative approaches to inquiry.

Looking to foster change beyond campus, critical qualitative scholars have also challenged their peers to actively participate in the governance and program planning of relevant professional organizations (for example, serving on the executive board or program committees of educational research associations, contributing to the collaborative authorship of organizational policy statements, or submitting constructive feedback) when organizational documents and proposed governance changes are posted for public comment (Koro-Ljungberg, Gemignani, Brodeur, and Kmiec, 2007; Lincoln and Cannella, 2004b). To interrupt the hegemonic knowledge regimes preserved by the editorial review process of academic journals, Stanley (2007) calls for critical scholars to actively engage in the development of editorial board training programs that "educate, raise the consciousness, take a stand, question and reframe . . . the troubling systems that perpetuate the master narrative" (p. 21).

The common thread connecting these institutional and organizational intervention strategies is a belief that critical qualitative scholars can and must facilitate change from within the very organizations that seek to marginalize them. As such, we concur with Giroux (2012) as he addresses the current educational crisis and ask scholars to think critically so they/we may act imaginatively as we intervene from within to foster educational equity and social change. The alternative, ceding the academic heartland to the architects and proponents of methodological conservatism, is inconsistent with an emancipatory approach, and the stakes are too high for both critical scholars and marginalized communities.

Intervention Through the Socialization of New Educational Researchers

Another strategy for confronting the escalating influence of methodological conservatism is to reconsider the norms and experiences that frame the socialization of educational researchers. Specifically, critical qualitative higher education scholars must engage in conversations with their campus colleagues about the way Colleges of Education teach research design and qualitative inquiry (Cannella and Lincoln, 2009; Gunzenhauser and Gerstl-Pepin, 2006; Koro-Ljungberg, 2007; Lather, 2006; Lincoln, 1998; Lincoln and Cannella, 2004b; O'Connor and O'Neill, 2004; Pallas, 2001). As Kezar (2004) proposes, "it is our responsibilities as teachers to have students read the philosophical texts referred to in methodology texts, and as scholars I believe we must also read and wrestle with these works if we want to improve the scholarship developed in this field" (p. 44). We contend that education faculty members, whether they are responsible for teaching methodology courses or not, must be encouraged to reflect on how their specific research orientations as well as their unique social identities serve to privilege certain bodies of knowledge while marginalizing others. Although it is naïve to expect all educational scholars to openly embrace the principles of critical methodology (indeed, we recognize the right of educational researchers to formulate methodological commitments congruent with a wide range of epistemological beliefs, including post/positivism), it is important for faculty to acknowledge that their scholarly identities shape, and in many ways constrain, the methodological possibilities imagined by doctoral students engaged in the process of formulating research agendas of their own. To be sure, these same doctoral students are the faculty, journal reviewers, and teachers of qualitative research in the future; the epistemological and methodological impact of introductions to qualitative inquiry has the potential to expand or be reified across generations.

Once faculty have reflected on their individual roles in shaping the methodological socialization of doctoral students, faculty colleagues have the potential to engage in a dialogue on the methodological norms and practices that frame their school's or department's doctoral curriculum in general and methodology coursework in particular. These conversations should not only take stock of contemporary pedagogical principles and practices but also work toward articulating a vision for a doctoral curriculum and institutional research culture that supports diverse epistemological perspectives. As Pallas (2001) notes "the issue of which epistemologies and whose get privileged in doctoral programs is a matter of politics and power" (p. 10). As a result, methodological conversations among faculty peers can be a source of conflict and controversy if these conversations are not grounded in mutual respect and an appreciation for the unique scholarly contributions of diverse epistemological and methodological perspectives. Such faculty conversations could include, how does a Native American graduate student deeply committed to the principles of indigenous epistemology and methodology navigate the power dynamics embedded in her relationship with a methodology professor who requires all students design and conduct a "standard" participant-observation research project? How may this graduate student account for and represent the power wielded by the faculty member in the research process? In class discussions, does the professor acknowledge the profound role her social identities, theoretical orientations, and research methodological principles play in privileging certain bodies of knowledge and marginalizing others?

In a 2001 Educational Researcher article describing the UC Riverside School of Education's attempt to reshape graduate preparation in educational research methods, Page (2001) applauds her school's decision to initiate dialogue in a four-member task force rather than a schoolwide faculty retreat, given that the task force dialogues served to "contain the conflict that could have easily erupted had discussions begun with faculty as a whole," as well as provided a rehearsal for the schoolwide discussions of methodological differences that followed. Regardless of whether conversations are initiated within a methodology task force, department faculty meetings, or schoolwide faculty retreats, the important step is to engage in dialogue. Avoiding discussions of epistemological and methodological difference for the sake of keeping the peace may provide a temporary sense of harmony, but this strategy holds dangerous long-term consequences as it serves to perpetuate the status quo, doctoral program curricula that marginalize critical methodological frameworks and undermine the potential for addressing issues of educational inequity via scholarly inquiry.

One possible outcome of individual and collaborative reflexive activities may be the realization that education faculty need to move critical methodological perspectives from the margins to the center of educational inquiry coursework. Rather than simply adding a "special week" on critical theory to the end of introductory research courses or offering special seminars on particular critical methodological frameworks for the few students interested in this type of inquiry, critical methodological perspectives and principles need to be fully integrated into introductory, intermediate, and advanced methodology courses. Better yet, they should be integrated across the entire doctoral curriculum including foundational studies and advanced thematic seminars. As such, students learn about the various epistemological perspectives of faculty across the department as they develop their own perspective.

In addition, congruent with the argument we make in "Confronting Qualitative Inquiry in Higher Education" regarding the importance of foregrounding issues of methodology rather than method in discussions of innovation in educational inquiry, we advocate for transforming traditional doctoral "methods requirements" into "methodological knowledge expectations." More specifically, rather than emphasizing the acquisition of specific data collection skills (for example, interviews, observation, and document analysis), doctoral coursework expectations need to map out a path for students to become familiar with the diverse epistemological and methodological frameworks that guide educational inquiry as well as cultivate their ability to design and carry out conceptually congruent research that links beliefs about the nature of knowledge to the selection or development of a particular inquiry framework.

In order to effectively counter the disciplining discourse regimes of academic capitalism and the scientifically based educational research movement, emerging critical higher education scholars must be able to articulate and defend the underlying assumptions and aims that guide their scholarship; questions of epistemology and methodology, not method. Accordingly, the socialization experiences of emerging critical educational researchers must also prepare students to engage in scholarly dialogues with proponents of methodological conservatism; a failure to do so will leave students ill-equipped to engage in dialogue and thereby may perpetuate the continued marginalization of nondominant epistemological perspectives and exacerbate conditions of educational inequity.

In addition to shifting the focus of doctoral level research socialization from method to methodology, critical qualitative higher education scholars would be well served by integrating coursework and conversations on the politics of inquiry into doctoral level research training. Conducting research, critical or otherwise, is a political act (Battiste, 2006). Rather than denying or lamenting the political nature of research in the academy, critical qualitative scholars need to actively engage in the politics of knowledge and cultivate the political competencies needed to survive and thrive in the academy. Huckaby (2007), Cheek (2008), and Lincoln and Cannella (2004b) discuss the importance of cultivating political competencies within the qualitative research community but stop short of naming specific political skills. Drawing from our own experiences within the academy and literature on grassroots activism (Kezar and Lester, 2011; Meyerson, 2008), we offer the following political competencies which may prove helpful in navigating the path to professional success and social justice research: networking and forming strategic alliances, teambuilding, fostering trust, lobbying, organizing, leadership, leveraging small wins, sharing information, interpersonal influence, collaboration, and negotiation.

Curricular strategies for cultivating political skills include assigning and discussing interdisciplinary texts (for example, leadership studies, management, peace studies, public policy, political science, social work) that shed light on the theories and practices of political activism; the development of assignments that ask students to critically analyze and respond to the disciplining discourses that frame documents such as the NRC's (2002) *Scientific Research in Education* or the *Standards for Reporting on Empirical Social Science Research in AERA Publications* (AERA, 2006); recruiting guest speakers to discuss their encounters with and strategies for resisting methodological conservatism in the higher education scholarly community; and engaging students in reflective dialogue on the behaviors and skills of successful (as well as not so successful) political leaders inside and outside of higher education. At the heart of this curricular recommendation is a belief that the development of meaningful resistance to the aims and principles of methodological conservatism requires an understanding of and ability to engage in the politics of knowledge production (Cheek, 2008). We contend that doctoral coursework is a critical forum for cultivating the skills, knowledge, and will to engage in the politics of inquiry.

Intervention Through Working and Speaking with Multiple Educational Research Constituencies

Inextricably connected, yet distinct, from the curricular recommendations we offered above, is the call for critical qualitative scholars to contest the advance of methodological conservatism by cultivating the ability and means to network with the multiple constituencies of educational research. To be sure, critical qualitative scholars are adept at engaging in scholarly critiques of the academic capitalism and scientifically based educational research regimes of truth. Commenting on early academic responses to the NRC's (2002) *Scientific Research in Education,* St. Pierre (2004) observed, "resistance has already begun to organize and will continue to do so as educational researchers accomplish the ethical work of investigating the power relations that are attempting to produce a small, impoverished scientific-based educational inquiry that shuts down any chances of that democracy to come" (p. 137). We reiterate the importance of dialogue between constituencies as stressed in the previous chapter. Engaging in constructive dialogue with other members of the educational research community via scholarly publications and conference symposia is an important strategy for contesting methodological conservatism, advancing and achieving the equity aims of critical qualitative scholarship.

In addition, critical inquiry necessitates dialogue and engagement with individuals, communities, and agencies located outside the academy (Apple, 2006a,

2006b; Greenwood and Levin, 2000, 2005; Koro-Ljungberg, Gemignani, Brodeur, and Kmiec, 2007; Lincoln and Cannella, 2004b). Apple (2006a, 2006b) contends that one of the reasons that architects of neoliberal and neoconservative educational agendas have been so successful in capturing the public's attention and support is their deployment of a sophisticated media strategy that facilitates the rapid and broad dissemination of conservative news, research, and opinions. If emerging and seasoned critical qualitative scholars wish to quell the advancement of methodological conservatism within the higher education research community, they (we) must develop the capacity to counter conservative attacks and proactively communicate their own equity agenda via diverse social media outlets (for example, editorials and letters to the editors, congressional testimony, policy briefs, community newsletters and presentations, press releases, web sites, podcasts, Facebook [FB], Twitter, radio and television interviews), much like how social media has provided alternative political and educational tools for massive demonstrations, protests, and information dissemination across the globe (Giroux, 2012).

For example, the Critical Lede (www.thecriticallede.com) is a series of podcasts designed by Drs. W. Benjamin Myers and Desiree D. Rowe. These communication professors regularly review qualitative articles and/or interview qualitative scholars and post the podcasts for download. You may also friend them on FB or follow them on Twitter. There are currently over 70 podcasts and interviews with scholars such as Drs. Norman Denzin, Henry Giroux, D. Soyini Madison, and Ron Pelias, dealing with critical topics such as graduate student socialization. In another example, multiple university and community constituencies have recently come together in "fullparticipation.net" in order to connect sets of conversations about change in higher education that often proceed separately, such as "people working under the umbrella of equity, diversity and inclusion with those working under the umbrella of community, public and civic engagement" ("Full participation," 2011, para. 1).

Further, to cultivate the broad communication network envisioned by Apple (2006a, 2006b), progressive scholars committed to the innovative methodological principles and practices described in the previous chapter must reimagine the socialization experiences of educational scholars, including educational inquiry coursework and continuing education opportunities sponsored by scholarly associations (Greenwood and Levin, 2000; Lincoln and Cannella, 2004b). Fine, Weis, Weseen, and Wong (2000) underscore the ethical imperative of expanding the scope of critical methodological training to include communication with diverse audiences as well as offer suggestions for the content of these new socialization experiences. The authors assert:

> *We exit this chapter with our fiercest injunction: that we have an ethical responsibility to retreat from the stance of dispassion all to prevalent in the academy and to educate our students toward analyzing, writing, and publishing in multiple genres at one and the same time—in policy talk, in the voices of empiricism, through the murky swamps of self-reflective "writing-stories," and in the more accessible language of pamphlets, fliers, and community booklets. That is, if we are serious about enabling our students to be fluent across methods, to be engaged with community struggles, and to theorize conditions of social (in)justice, we must recognize that flickers and movements for social change happen in varied sites— courtrooms, legislative offices, the media, community-based organizations, and church groups, as well as the academy—and therefore through varied texts [p. 128].*

Specific strategies for cultivating expanded communication skills include enrolling in journalism, public relations, and community writing workshops and courses sponsored by media organizations, university extension programs, and professional associations. In addition, critical education scholars could make time for reading texts other than peer-reviewed journals and academic manuscripts. Regularly reading editorials, policy briefs, and press releases will enhance understanding of various communication tools and sharpen abilities to articulate concise and compelling arguments that speak to multiple audiences. As such, critical qualitative scholars dedicated to engaging in transformational scholarship must be prepared, committed, and able to engage in collaborative inquiry and political action on multiple fronts. Realizing this goal necessitates fundamental changes in the socialization, training, and evaluation of educational researchers.

Conclusion

We recognize that the recommendations and strategies discussed above are time and energy intensive. Indeed, Strega (2005) acknowledges the difficult challenge of "steering a course between the conflicting demands of personal, political, and community commitments and the academic and professional 'standards' to which we make ourselves subject if we choose to pursue our work within the academy and other mainstream structures" (p. 227). Without a doubt, actively engaging in efforts to expand one's understandings of emancipatory epistemologies, become social media savvy, transform educational inquiry curricula, and initiate change from within organizations as members of influential committees while simultaneously meeting traditional promotion and tenure expectations is emotionally and physically exhausting work. We contend, however, it is far more costly to perpetuate dominant traditions of qualitative inquiry that fail to address the fundamental philosophical underpinnings of in/equity in higher education. We encourage critical qualitative scholars to explore, develop, and intervene through multidimensional relationships between themselves and students, faculty, institutions, community partners, and various local, regional, national, and/or global constituencies.

Our objective in calling attention to the oppressive norms of academic capitalism and the narrow standards of legitimate inquiry embedded in calls for scientific educational research is not to discourage higher education scholars from engaging in social justice research informed by non-dominant epistemological and methodological perspectives; indeed our goal is quite the opposite. We are optimistic that productive resistance and change is possible within and beyond the academy; however, it is imperative that critical qualitative scholars grasp an understanding of the obstacles they/we are likely to encounter along the journey so they/we may make informed decisions throughout intervention processes.

This monograph has attempted to map the terrain of higher education qualitative inquiry, shedding light on the conservative ideologies seeking to constrain innovation, inflict a façade of clarity and reproduce the status quo. Although sweeping topographical change is not likely to occur in the immediate future, critical qualitative higher education researchers can and do engage in meaningful resistance from positions on the margins of the academy. As Kouritzin, Piquemal, and Norman (2008) remind us, "it is possible to 'blur the edges' a little, while still being pragmatic in terms of playing by the rules" (p. 3). This blurring of the edges has an ongoing impact on the very systems we wish to change, potentially altering the systems of logic that make in/equity possible—visible even—in contemporary higher education.

Critical qualitative inquiry toward educational equity need not always be about immediate large revolution in terms of the grand sense of things, but may happen through daily practices of intervention. Small steps that build toward radical transformation cannot be underestimated. We invite both emerging and seasoned critical higher education scholars to interrupt the violence of methodological clarity and answer the call to action articulated in this chapter through contributions to cumulative social change and educational equity.

Notes

1. Denzin and Lincoln (2005b) have identified and defined eight moments in qualitative research. These moments include the *traditional* (1900–1950); the *modernist* or golden age (1950–1970), *blurred genres* (1970–1986); *the crisis of representation* (1986–1990); the *postmodern* (1990–1995); *post-experimental inquiry* (1995–2000); the *methodologically contested present* (2000–2004); and the *fractured future* (2005–present). Although temporal in their explanation, it is imperative to understand that each moment continues to operate across a broad qualitative project today.

2. "Hir" and "ze" are commonly used pronouns that are inclusive of transgender and gender transgressive people in our communities and will be used throughout this document.

3. A decade has also passed since the passage of the *No Child Left Behind Act of 2001* and *the Education Sciences Reform Act of 2002* which also codified the principles of scientific educational research.

4. This legislation established funding for state initiatives that draw upon scientifically based research to improve student reading and reading-related instructional practices.

5. Hackett (1990) used the term *academic capitalism* to describe significant structural changes in academic science.

References

Abes, E., and Kasch, D. (2007). Using queer theory to explore lesbian college students' multiple dimensions of identity. *Journal of College Student Development, 48*(6), 619–636.

Alemán, E. Jr., Salazar, T., Rorrer, A., and Parker, L. (2011). Introduction to postracialism in U.S. public school and higher education settings: The politics of education in the age of Obama. *Peabody Journal of Education, 86*(5), 478–487.

Althusser, L. (1971). *Lenin and philosophy, and other essays* (B. Brewster, Trans.). New York: Monthly Review Press.

American Civil Rights Institute. (n.d.). *About us.* Sacramento, CA: American Civil Rights Institute. Retrieved July 15, 2011, from http://www.acri.org/about.html.

American Educational Research Association (AERA). (2006). *Standards for reporting on empirical social science research in AERA publications.* Retrieved July 15, 2011, from http://www.aera.net/uploadedFiles/Publications/Journals/Educational_Researcher/3506/12ERv35n6_Standard4Report%20.pdf.

American Educational Research Association (AERA). (2008). *Definition of Scientifically Based Research.* Retrieved July 15, 2011, from http://www.aera.net/uploadedFiles/Opportunities/DefinitionofScientificallyBasedResearch.pdf.

American Educational Research Association (AERA). (2009). *Standards for reporting on humanities-oriented research in AERA publications.* Retrieved July 15, 2011, from http://www.aera.net/uploadedFiles/Journals_and_Publications/Journals/481-486_09EDR09.pdf.

Anyon, J. (2006). What should count as educational research: Notes toward a new paradigm. In G. Ladson-Billings and W. F. Tate (Eds.), *Education research in the public interest* (pp. 17–26). New York: Teachers College Press.

Apple, M. W. (2006a). Educating the "right" way: Markets, standard, God, and inequality (2nd ed.). New York: Routledge.

Apple, M. W. (2006b). Interrupting the Right: On doing critical educational work in conservative times. In G. Ladson-Billings and W. F. Tate. (Eds.), *Education research in the public interest: Social justice, action, and policy* (pp. 27–45.) New York: Teachers College Press.

Atkinson, P., and others (Eds.). (2001). *Handbook of ethnography.* Thousand Oaks, CA: Sage.

Ayers, D. F. (2005). Neoliberal ideology in community college mission statements. *Review of Higher Education, 28*(4), 527–549.

Barad, K. (2008). Posthumanist performativity: Toward an understanding of how matter comes to matter. In S. Alaimo and S. Hekman (Eds.), *Material feminisms* (pp. 120–154). Bloomington, IN: Indiana Press.

Bartik, T. J. (2005). Increasing the economic development benefits of higher education in Michigan. *Journal of Workforce Development, 1*(1), 19–28.

Battiste, M. (2006, May). The global challenge: Research ethics for protecting Indigenous knowledge and heritage. Keynote address at the Congress of Qualitative Inquiry. Urbana-Champaign, IL.

Battiste, M. (2008). Research ethics for protecting Indigenous knowledge and heritage: Institutional and researcher responsibilities. In N. K. Denzin, Y. S. Lincoln, and L. Smith (Eds.), *Handbook of critical and Indigenous methodologies* (pp. 497–510). Thousand Oaks, CA: Sage.

Bennoff, R. J. (2010, September). Proposed federal R&D funding for FY 2011 dips to $143 Billion, with cuts in national defense R&D (InfoBrief NSF 10-327). Washington, DC: National Science Foundation. Retrieved July 15, 2011, from http://www.nsf.gov/ statistics/infbrief/ nsf10327/.

Best, S., and Kellner, D. (1991). *Postmodern theory*. New York: Guilford Press.

Bijian, Z. (2005). China's "peaceful rise" to great-power status. *Foreign Affairs, 84*(5), 18–24.

Blake, E. C. (2002). Spatiality past and present: An interview with Edward Soja. *Social Archaeology, 2*, 139–158.

Bloch, M. (2004). A discourse that disciplines, governs, and regulates: The National Research Council's Report on Scientific Research in Education. *Qualitative Inquiry, 10*(1), 96–110.

Bloom, L. R. (1998). *Under the sign of hope: Feminist methodology and narrative interpretation*. Albany, NY: SUNY Press.

Bloom, L. R. (2009). Introduction: Global perspectives on poverty and social justice. *International Journal of Qualitative Studies in Education, 22*(3), 333–351.

Bogdan, R., and Biklen, S. K. (2006). *Qualitative research for education: An introduction to theories and methods* (5th ed.). Boston: Allyn and Bacon.

Bok, D. (2003). *Universities in the marketplace: The commercialization of higher education*. Princeton, NJ: Princeton University Press.

Brandl, J., and Weber, V. (1995). *An agenda for reform: Competition, community, concentration*. Minneapolis: Office of the Governor.

Brayboy, B. M. J. (2004). Hiding in the ivy: American Indian students and visibility in elite educational settings. *Harvard Educational Review, 74*(2), 125–152.

Brinkmann, S. (2011). Interviewing and the production of the conversational self. In N. Denzin and M. Giardina (Eds.), *Qualitative inquiry and global crises* (pp. 56–75). Walnut Creek, CA: Left Coast Press.

Broadhead, L., and Howard, S. (1998). "The art of punishing": The research assessment exercise and the ritualisation of power in higher education. *Education Policy Analysis Archives, 6*(8), 1–11.

Broido, E., and Manning, K. (2002). Philosophical foundations and current theoretical perspectives in qualitative research. *Journal of College Student Development, 43*(4), 434–445.

Brown, C. (2009). Democracy's friend or foe? The effects of recent IMF conditional lending in Latin America. *International Political Science Review, 30*(4), 431–457.

Brown, L., and Strega, S. (Eds.). (2005). *Research as resistance: Critical, indigenous, and anti-oppressive approaches.* Toronto, ON: Canadian Scholars Press.

Brydon-Miller, M., and others. (2011). Jazz and the bayan tree: Roots and riffs on participatory action research. In N. K. Denzin and Y. S. Lincoln (Eds.), *The Sage handbook of qualitative research* (4th ed., pp. 387–400). Thousand Oaks, CA: Sage.

Burbules, N. C., and Torres, C. A. (2000). Globalization and education: An introduction. In N. C. Burbules and C. A. Torres (Eds.), *Globalization and education: Critical perspectives* (pp. 1–26). New York: Routledge.

Burke, J. C. (2005). Preface. In J. C. Burke (Ed.), *Achieving accountability in higher education: Balancing public, academic, and market demands* (pp. ix–xix). San Francisco: Jossey-Bass.

Butler, C. (2002). *Postmodernism: A very short introduction.* Oxford, UK: Oxford University Press.

Cameron, D. (2001). *Working with spoken discourse.* Thousand Oaks, CA: Sage.

Cannella, G. S. (2004). Regulatory power: Can a feminist poststructuralist engage in research oversight? *Qualitative Inquiry, 10*(2), 235–245.

Cannella, G. S., and Lincoln, Y. S. (2004a). Dangerous discourses II: Comprehending and countering the redeployment of discourses (and resources) in the generation of liberatory inquiry. *Qualitative Inquiry, 10*(2), 165–174.

Cannella, G. S., and Lincoln, Y. S. (2004b). Epilogue: Claiming a critical public social science—Reconceptualizing and redeploying research. *Qualitative Inquiry, 10*(2), 298–309.

Cannella, G. S., and Lincoln, Y. S. (2007). Predatory vs. dialogic ethics: Constructing an illusion or ethical practice as the core of research methods. *Qualitative Inquiry, 13*(3), 315–335.

Cannella, G. S., and Lincoln, Y. S. (2009). Deploying qualitative methods for critical social purposes. In N. K. Denzin and M. D. Giardina (Eds.), *Qualitative inquiry and social justice* (pp. 53–80). Walnut Creek, CA: Left Coast Press.

Carducci, R., and others. (2007, November). A dialogue on the role of critical inquiry in (re)shaping the public agenda for higher education. Symposium presented at the Association for the Study of Higher Education, Louisville, KY.

Charmaz, K. (2000) Grounded Theory: Objectivist and Constructivist Methods. In N. K. Denzin and Y. S. Lincoln (Eds.), *The Sage handbook of qualitative research* (2nd ed., pp. 509–535). Thousand Oaks, CA: Sage.

Charmaz, K. (2005). Grounded theory in the 21st century: Applications for advancing social justice theory. In N. K. Denzin and Y. Lincoln (Eds.), *The Sage handbook of qualitative research* (3rd ed., pp. 507–535). Thousand Oaks, CA: Sage.

Chase, S. E. (2005). Narrative inquiry: Multiple lenses, approaches, voices. In N. K. Denzin and Y. S. Lincoln (Eds.), *The Sage handbook of qualitative research* (3rd ed., pp. 651–679). Thousand Oaks, CA: Sage.

Chaudhry, L. N. (2000). Researching "my people," researching myself: Fragments of a reflexive tale. In E. St. Pierre and W. Pillow (Eds.), *Working the ruins: Feminist poststructural theory* (pp. 96–113). New York: Routledge.

Cheek, J. (2005). The practice and politics of funded qualitative research. *The Sage handbook of qualitative research* (3rd ed., pp. 387–409). Thousand Oaks, CA: Sage.

Cheek, J. (2007). Qualitative inquiry, ethics, and politics of evidence: Working within these spaces rather than being worked over by them. *Qualitative Inquiry, 13*(8), 1051–1059.

Cheek, J. (2008). A fine line: Positioning qualitative inquiry in the wake of the politics of evidence. *International Review of Qualitative Research, 1*(1), 19–32.

Chesler, M., Lewis, A., and Crowfoot, J. (2005). *Challenging racism in higher education.* New York: Rowman and Littlefield.

Chomsky, N. (2004). *Chomsky on mis-education.* New York: Rowman.

Clarke, A. E. (2005). *Situational analysis: Grounded theory after the postmodern turn.* Thousand Oaks, CA: Sage.

Clarke, A. E. (2007). Feminisms, grounded theory, and situational analysis. In S. N. Hesse-Biber and P. L. Leavy (Eds.), *Feminist research practice: A primer* (pp. 345–370). Thousand Oaks, CA: Sage.

Clough, P. T. (2007). *The affective turn: Theorizing the social.* Durham, NC: Duke University Press.

Colyar, J. (2006, November). Becoming through writing: Translating research in understanding of self and the world. Paper presented at the Association for the Study of Higher Education, Anaheim, CA.

Common Rule, 45 CFR 46.107 (1991).

Cook, T. D. (2002). Randomized experiments in educational policy research: A critical examination of the reasons the educational evaluation community has offered for not doing them. *Educational Evaluation and Policy Analysis, 24*(3), 175–199.

Cook, T. D. (2003). Why have educational evaluators chosen not to do randomized experiments? *Annals of the American Academy of Political and Social Science, 589*(1), 114–149.

Corbin, J., and Strauss, A. (2008). *Basics of qualitative research: Techniques and procedures for developing grounded theory* (3rd ed.). Thousand Oaks, CA: Sage.

Creswell, J. W. (2007). *Qualitative inquiry and research design: Choosing among five approaches* (2nd ed.). Thousand Oaks, CA: Sage.

Creswell, J. W. (2011a). Controversies in mixed methods research. In N. K. Denzin and Y. S. Lincoln (Eds.), *The Sage handbook of qualitative research* (4th ed., pp. 269–283). Thousand Oaks, CA: Sage.

Creswell, J. W. (2011b). *Educational research: Planning, conducting and evaluating quantitative and qualitative research* (4th ed.). New York: Pearson.

Creswell, J. W., Carroll Klassan, A., Plano Clark, V. L., and Clegg Smith, K. (2011). *Best practices for mixed methods research in the health sciences.* Washington, DC: National Institutes of Health. Retrieved July 15, 2011, from http://obssr.od.nih.gov/scientific_areas/methodology /mixed_methods_research/index.aspx.

Crotty, M. J. (1998). *The foundations of social research: Meaning and perspective in the research process.* Thousand Oaks, CA: Sage.

Curtis, B. (2008). The performance-based research fund: Research assessment and funding in New Zealand. *Globalisation, Societies and Education, 6*(2), 179–194.

Daiute, C., and Lightfoot, C. (2004). Editors' introduction: Theory and craft in narrative inquiry. In C. Daiute and C. Lightfoot (Eds.), *Narrative analysis: Studying the development of individuals in society* (pp. vii–xviii). Thousand Oaks, CA: Sage.

DeCarvalho, F.J.C. (2002). Strengthening the defenses of the Brazilian economy against external vulnerability. *International Journal of Political Economy, 32*(4), 35–48.

Dee, J. (2006). Institutional autonomy and state-level accountability: Loosely coupled governance and the public good. In W. G. Tierney (Ed.), *Governance and the public good* (pp. 133–156). Albany, NY: State University of New York Press.

Denzin, N. K. (2003). *Performance ethnography: Critical pedagogy and the politics of culture.* Thousand Oaks, CA: Sage.

Denzin, N. K. (2009). The elephant in the living room: Or extending the conversation about the politics of evidence. *Qualitative Research, 9*(2), 139–160.

Denzin, N. K. (2010a). On elephants and gold standards. *Qualitative Research, 10*(2), 269–272.

Denzin, N. K. (2010b). *The qualitative manifesto: A call to arms.* Walnut Creek: Left Coast Press.

Denzin, N. K. (2011). The politics of evidence. In N. K. Denzin and Y. S. Lincoln (Eds.). *The Sage handbook of qualitative research* (4th ed., pp. 645–657). Thousand Oaks, CA: Sage.

Denzin, N. K., and Giardina, M. D. (2006). Introduction: Qualitative inquiry and the conservative challenge. In N. K. Denzin and M. D. Giardina (Eds.), *Qualitative inquiry and the conservative challenge* (pp. ix–xxxi). Walnut Creek, CA: Left Coast Press.

Denzin, N. K., and Giardina, M. D. (2009). Qualitative inquiry and social justice: Toward a politics of hope. In N. K. Denzin and M. D. Giardina (Eds.), *Qualitative inquiry and social justice* (pp. 11–52). Walnut Creek, CA: Left Coast Press.

Denzin, N. K., and Giardina, M. D. (2010). Introduction. In N. Denzin and M. Giardina (Eds.), *Qualitative inquiry and human rights* (pp. 13–41). Walnut Creek: Left Coast Press.

Denzin, N. K., and Lincoln, Y. S. (Eds.). (1994). *The Sage handbook of qualitative research.* Thousand Oaks: Sage.

Denzin, N. K., and Lincoln, Y. S. (Eds.). (2000) *The Sage handbook of qualitative research* (2nd ed.). Thousand Oaks: Sage.

Denzin, N. K., and Lincoln, Y. (2005a). Introduction: The discipline and practice of qualitative research. In N. K. Denzin and Y. S. Lincoln (Eds.), *The Sage handbook of qualitative research* (3rd ed., pp. 1–33). Thousand Oaks, CA: Sage.

Denzin, N. K., and Lincoln, Y. S. (Eds.). (2005b). *The Sage handbook of qualitative research.* (3rd ed.). Thousand Oaks: Sage.

Denzin, N. K., and Lincoln, Y. S. (Eds.). (2011). *The Sage handbook of qualitative research.* (4th ed.). Thousand Oaks, CA: Sage.

Dillard, C. (2000). The substance of things hoped for, the evidence of things not seen: Examining an endarkened feminist epistemology in educational research and leadership. *Qualitative Studies in Education, 13*(6), 661–681.

Eckel, P. D., Couturier, L., and Luu, D. T. (2005). *Peering around the bend: The leadership challenges of privatization, accountability, and market-based state policy.* Washington, DC: American Council on Education.

Education Sciences Reform Act, 108 Cong. 2nd Sess. 48 (2002).

Emerson, R. M., Fretz, R. L., and Shaw, L. L. (1995). *Writing ethnographic fieldnotes.* Chicago: University of Chicago Press.

Esterberg, K. G. (2002). *Qualitative methods in social research* (1st ed.). New York: McGraw-Hill.

Etzkowitz, H., Webster, A., and Healey, P. (Eds.). (1998). *Capitalizing knowledge: New intersections of industry and academia.* Albany, NY: State University of New York.

Fairclough, N. (2001). The discourse of new labour: Critical discourse analysis. In M. Wetherell, S. Taylor, and S. J. Yates (Eds.), *Discourse as data: A guide for analysis* (pp. 229–266). Thousand Oaks, CA: Sage.

Fine, M. (1994). Working the hyphens: Reinventing self and other in qualitative research. In N. K. Denzin and Y. S. Lincoln (Eds.), *The Sage handbook of qualitative research* (pp. 70–82). Thousand Oaks, CA: Sage.

Fine, M., Weis, L., Weseen, S., and Wong, L. (2000). For whom? Qualitative research, representations, and social responsibilities. In N. K. Denzin and Y. S. Lincoln (Eds.), *The Sage handbook of qualitative* research (2nd ed., pp. 107–131). Thousand Oaks, CA: Sage.

Finley, S. (2011). Critical arts-based inquiry: The pedagogy and performance of a radical ethical aesthetic. In N. K. Denzin and Y. S. Lincoln (Eds.). *The Sage handbook of qualitative research* (4th ed., pp. 435–450). Thousand Oaks, CA: Sage.

Foley, D., and Valenzuela, A. (2005). Critical ethnography: The politics of collaboration. In N. K. Denzin and Y. S. Lincoln (Eds.), *The Sage handbook of qualitative research* (3rd ed., pp. 217–235). Thousand Oaks, CA: Sage.

Fontana, A., and Prokos, A. H. (2007). *The interview: From formal to postmodern.* Walnut Creek, CA: Left Coast Press.

Foucault, M. (1980). Truth and power. (C. Gordon, L. Marshall, J. Mepham, K. Soper, Trans.) In C. Gordon. (Ed.), *Power/knowledge: Selected interviews and other writings 1972–1977* (pp. 109–133). New York: Pantheon.

Foucault, M. (1983). On the genealogy of ethics. In H. Dreyfus and P. Rabinow (Eds.), *Michel Foucault: Beyond structuralism and hermeneutics* (2nd ed., pp. 231–232). Chicago: University of Chicago Press.

Foucault, M. (1984). Nietzsche, geneaology, history. In P. Rabinow (Ed.), *The Foucault reader* (pp. 76–100). New York: Pantheon.

Foucault, M. (1987). Polemics, politics, and problematisations: An interview with Michel Foucault. In P. Rabinow (Ed.), *Michel Foucault: Ethics, subjectivity, truth* (pp. 113–119). New York: New Press.

Foucault, M. (1997). On the geneaology of ethics. In P. Rabinow (Ed.), *Ethics: subjectivity and truth* (pp. 253–280). New York: New Press.

Fraser, N. (1981). Foucault on modern power: Empirical insights and normative confusions. *PRAXIS International, 31*, 272–287.

Full participation: Building the architecture for diversity and public engagement on campus. Retrieved July 15, 2011, from fullparticipation.net.

Gibbs, P., Costley, C., Armsby, P., and Trakakis, A. (2007). Developing the ethics of worker-researchers through phronesis. *Teaching in Higher Education, 12*(3), 365–375.

Giddings. L. S. (2006, May). Mixed-methods research: Positivism dressed in drag? *Journal of Research in Nursing, 11*(3), 195–203.

Gildersleeve, R. E. (2010). *Fracturing opportunity: Mexican migrant students and college-going literacy.* New York: Peter Lang.

Gildersleeve, R. E. (2011, April). *Spotlight Session: Critical inquiry, disaster, and hope: New Orleans, LA.* Discussant comments presented at the American Educational Research Association, New Orleans, LA.

Gildersleeve, R., and Kuntz, A. (2011). A dialogue on space and method in qualitative research on education. *Qualitative Inquiry, 17*(1), 15–22.

Gildersleeve, R. E., Kuntz, A. M., Pasque, P. A., and Carducci, R. (2010). The role of critical inquiry in (re)constructing the public agenda for higher education: Confronting the conservative modernization of the academy. *Review of Higher Education, 34*(1), 85–121.

Gilgun, J. F. (2008). Lived experience, reflexivity, and research on perpetrators of interpersonal violence. *Qualitative Social Work, 7*(2), 181–197.

Gilgun, J. F. (2010). Reflexivity and qualitative research. *Current Issues in Qualitative Research, 1*(2), 1–31.

Giroux, H. A. (2001). *Theory and resistance in education: Towards a pedagogy for the opposition.* Westport, CT: Bergin and Garvey.

Giroux, H. A. (2012). *Education and the crisis of public values: Challenging the assault on teachers, students, and public education.* New York: Peter Lang.

Giroux, H. A., and Giroux, S. S. (2004). *Take back higher education: Race, youth, and the crisis of democracy in the post-civil rights era.* New York: Palgrave Macmillan.

Glaser, B. G., and Strauss, A. L. (1967). *Discovery of grounded theory: Strategies for qualitative research.* Chicago: Aldine.

Gottlieb, P. D., and Fogarty, M. (2003). Educational attainment and metropolitan growth. *Economic Development Quarterly, 17*(4), 325–336.

Greenwood, D. J., and Levin, M. (2000). Reconstructing the relationships between universities and society through action research. In N. K. Denzin and Y. S. Lincoln (Eds.), *Handbook of qualitative research* (2nd ed., pp. 85–106). Thousand Oaks, CA: Sage.

Greenwood, D. J., and Levin, M. (2005). Reform of the social sciences, and of universities through action research. In N. K. Denzin and Y. S. Lincoln (Eds.), *The Sage handbook of qualitative research* (3rd ed., pp. 43–64). Thousand Oaks, CA: Sage.

Griffin, K. A., and Museus, S. D. (Eds.). (2011). Using mixed-methods approaches to studying intersectionality in higher education. *New Directions for Institutional Research,* No. 151. San Francisco: Jossey-Bass.

Guba, E. G., and Lincoln, Y. S. (2005). Paradigmatic controversies, contradictions, and emerging confluences. In N. K Denzin and Y. S. Lincoln (Eds.), *The Sage handbook of qualitative research* (3rd ed., pp. 191–215). Thousand Oaks, CA: Sage.

Guido, F. (2011). Life stories of the daughter of first-generation Italian immigrants. In P. A. Pasque and M. Errington Nicholson (Eds.), *Empowering women in higher education and student affairs: Theory, research, narratives and practice from feminist perspectives* (pp. 163–177). Sterling, VA: Stylus/American College Personnel Association.

Gunzenhauser, M. G. (2006). A moral epistemology of knowing subjects: Theorizing a relational turn for qualitative research. *Qualitative Inquiry, 12*(3), 621–647.

Gunzenhauser, M. G. and Gerstl-Pepin, C. I. (2006). Engaging graduate education: A pedagogy for epistemological and theoretical diversity. *Review of Higher Education, 29*(3), 319–346.

Hackett, E. J. (1990). Science as a vocation in the 1990s: The changing organizational culture of academic science. *The Journal of Higher Education, 61*(3), 241–279.

Hammersley, M., and Atkinson, P. (2007). *Ethnography: Principles in practice* (3rd ed.). New York: Routledge.

Hardiman, R., and Jackson, B. (2007). Conceptual foundations for social justice education: Conceptual overview. In M. Adams, L. A. Bell, and P. Griffin (Eds.), *Teaching for diversity and social justice* (pp. 35–66). New York: Routledge.

Hare, P. G. (2003). The United Kingdom's Education research assessment exercise: Impact on institutions, departments, individuals. *Higher Management and Policy, 15*(2), 43–62.

Harro, B. (2000a). The cycle of liberation. In M. Adams, W. Blumenfeld, C. Castaneda, H. W. Hackman, M. L. Peters, and X. Zuniga (Eds.), *Readings for diversity and social justice* (pp. 463–469). New York: Routledge.

Harro, B. (2000b). The cycle of socialization. In M. Adams, W. Blumenfeld, C. Castaneda, H. W. Hackman, M. L. Peters, and X. Zuniga (Eds.), *Readings for diversity and social justice* (pp. 15–20). New York: Routledge.

Hart, C. (1998). *Doing a literature review: Releasing the social science research imagination.* Thousand Oaks, CA: Sage.

Hart, J. (2006). Women and feminism in higher education scholarship: An analysis of three core journals. *Journal of Higher Education, 77*(1), 40–61.

Hesse-Biber, S. N. (2007a). Feminist research: Exploring the interconnections of epistemology, methodology, and method. In S. N. Hesse-Biber and P. L. Leavy (Eds.), *Feminist research practice: A primer* (pp. 1–26). Thousand Oaks, CA: Sage.

Hesse-Biber, S. N. (2007b). The practice of feminist in-depth interviewing. In S. N. Hesse-Biber and P. L. Leavy (Eds.), *Feminist research practice: A primer* (pp. 111–148). Thousand Oaks, CA: Sage.

hooks, b., and West, C. (1991). *Breaking bread: Insurgent black intellectual life.* Boston: South End Press.

hooks, b. (1993). Eros, eroticism, and the pedagogical process. *Cultural Studies, 7*(1), 58–63.

hooks, b. (1998). *Teaching to transgress: Education as the practice of freedom.* New York: Routledge.

Howe, K. (2008). Isolating science from the humanities: The third dogma of educational research. In M. Giardina and N. Denzin (Eds.), *Qualitative research and the politics of evidence* (pp. 97–118). Walnut Creek, CA: Left Coast Press.

Howe, K. R. (2009). Positivist dogmas, rhetoric, and the education science question. *Educational Researcher, 38*(6), 428–440.

Huckaby, M. F. (2007). A conversation on practices of the self within relations of power: For scholars who speak dangerous truths. *International Journal of Qualitative Studies in Education, 20*(5), 513–529.

Husserl, E. (1931). *Ideas: General introduction to pure phenomenology* (D. Carr, Trans.). Evanston, IL: Northwestern University Press.

Husserl, E. (1970). *The crisis of European sciences and transcendental phenomenology* (D. Carr, Trans.). Evanston, IL: Northwestern University Press.

Hutchinson, S. R., and Lovell, C. D. (2004). A review of methodological characteristics of research published in key journals in higher education: Implications for graduate research training. *Research in Higher Education, 45*(4), 383–403.

Ibarra, R. (2006). Context diversity: Reframing higher education in the 21st century. In B. Holland and J. Meeropol (Eds.), *A more perfect vision: The future of campus engagement.* Providence, RI: Campus Compact. Retrieved April 18, 2011, from http://www.compact .org/community-members/context-diversity-reframing-higher-education-in-the-21st-century/4227/?zoom_highlight=ibarra.

Ikenberry, S. O. (2009). Privatizing the public research university. In C. C. Morphew and P. D. Eckel (Eds.), *Privatizing the public university: Perspectives across the academy* (pp. 1–6). Baltimore, MD: Johns Hopkins University Press.

Jackson, A. Y., and Mazzei, L. A. (Eds.). (2009). *Voice in qualitative inquiry: Challenging conventional, interpretive, and critical conceptions in qualitative research.* London: Routledge.

Johnson, R. B., and Onwuegbuzie, A. J. (2004). Mixed methods research: A research paradigm whose time has come. *Educational Researcher, 33*(7), 14–26.

Johnson, T. S. (2008). Qualitative research in question: A narrative of disciplinary power within the IRB. *Qualitative Inquiry, 14*(2), 212–232.

Johnstone, B. (2002). *Discourse analysis.* Malden, MA: Blackwell.

Jones, S. R., Torres, V., and Arminio, J. (2006). *Negotiating the complexities of qualitative research in higher education: Fundamental elements and issues.* New York: Routledge.

Kezar, A. J. (2004). Wrestling with philosophy: Improving scholarship in higher education. *Journal of Higher Education, 75*(1), 42–55.

Kezar, A., Gallant, T. B., Lester, J. (2011). Everyday people making a difference on college campuses: The tempered grassroots leadership tactics of faculty and staff. *Studies in Higher Education, 36*(2), 129–151.

Kezar, A., and Lester, J. (2011). *Enhancing campus capacity for leadership: An examination of grassroots leaders in higher education.* Stanford, CA: Stanford University Press.

Kincheloe, J. (2005). *Critical pedagogy: A primer.* New York: Peter Lang.

Kincheloe, J. L., and McLaren, P. (2005). Rethinking critical theory and qualitative research. In N. K. Denzin and Y. S. Lincoln (Eds.), *The Sage handbook of qualitative research* (3rd ed., pp. 303–342). Thousand Oaks, CA: Sage.

Kirp, D. L. (2003). *Shakespeare, Einstein, and the bottom line: The marketing of higher education.* Cambridge, MA: Harvard University Press.

Koro-Ljungberg, M. (2007). "Democracy to come": A personal narrative of pedagogical practices and "Othering" within a context of higher education and research training. *Teaching in Higher Education, 12*(5/6), 735–747.

Koro-Ljungberg, M., Gemignani, M., Brodeur, C. W., and Kmiec, C. (2007). The technologies of normalization and self: Thinking about IRBs and extrinsic research ethics with Foucault. *Qualitative Inquiry, 13*(8), 1075–1094.

Kouritzin, S. G., Piquemal, N.A.C., and Norman, R. (2008). *Qualitative research: Challenging the orthodoxies in standard academic discourse(s).* New York: Routledge.

Krugman, P. (2009). *The return of depression economics and the crisis of 2008.* New York: Norton.

Kuntz, A. (2009). Turning from time to space: Conceptualizing faculty work. In J. Smart (Ed.), *Higher education: Handbook of theory and research* (pp. 355–388). New York: Springer.

Lather, P. (1993). Fertile obsession: Validity after poststructuralism. *Sociological Quarterly, 34*(4), 673–693.

Lather, P. (1995). The validity of angels: Interpretive and textual strategies in researching the lives of women with HIV/AIDS. *Qualitative Inquiry, 1*(1) 41–68.

Lather, P. (2003). Issues of validity in openly ideological research: Between a rock and a soft place. In Y. S. Lincoln and N. K. Denzin (Eds.), *Turning points in qualitative research: Tying knots in a handkerchief* (pp. 185–215). Walnut Creek, CA: AltaMira Press.

Lather, P. (2004). This is your father's paradigm: Government intrusion and the case of qualitative research in education. *Qualitative Inquiry, 10*(1), 15–34.

Lather, P. (2006). Paradigm proliferation as a good thing to think with: Teaching qualitative research as a wild profusion. *Qualitative Studies in Education, 19*(1), 35–57.

Lather, P. (2007). *Getting lost: Feminist efforts toward a double(d) science.* Albany, NY: State University of New York Press.

Levin, J. S. (2007). *Nontraditional students and community colleges: The conflict of justice and neoliberalism.* New York: Palgrave Macmillan.

Lincoln, Y. S. (1998). The ethics of teaching in qualitative research. *Qualitative Inquiry, 4*(3), 315–327.

Lincoln, Y. S. (2005). Institutional review boards and methodological conservatism: The challenge to and from phenomenological paradigms. In N. K. Denzin and Y. S. Lincoln (Eds.), *The Sage handbook of qualitative research* (3rd ed., pp. 165–181). Thousand Oaks, CA: Sage.

Lincoln, Y. S. (2010). "What a long, strange trip it's been . . .": Twenty-five years of qualitative and new paradigm research. *Qualitative Inquiry, 16*(1), 3–9.

Lincoln, Y. S., and Cannella, G. S. (2004a). Dangerous discourses: Methodological conservatism and governmental regimes of truth. *Qualitative Inquiry, 10*(1), 5–14.

Lincoln, Y. S., and Cannella, G. S. (2004b). Qualitative research, power, and the radical right. *Qualitative Inquiry, 10*(2), 175–201.

Lincoln, Y. S., and Tierney, W. G. (2004). Qualitative research and institutional review boards. *Qualitative Inquiry, 10*(2), 219–234.

Madison, D. S. (2011). *Critical ethnography: Method, ethics, and performance* (2nd ed.). Thousand Oaks, CA: Sage.

Mahbubani, K. (2005). Understanding China. *Foreign Affairs, 84*(5), 49–60.

Marcus, G. E., and Fischer, M. M. (1999). *Anthropology as cultural critique: An experimental moment in the human sciences* (2nd ed.). Chicago: University of Chicago Press.

Marshall, C., and Rossman, G. B. (2011). *Designing qualitative research.* (5th ed.). Thousand Oaks, CA: Sage.

Marshall, J. (2007). Michel Foucault: Educational research as problematisation. In M. Peters and T. Besley (Eds.), *Why Foucault?* New Directions in Educational Research (pp. 15–28). New York: Peter Lang.

Massey, D. (1996). Politicising space and place. *Scottish Geographical Journal, 112,* 117–123.

Massey, D. (2005). *For space.* Thousand Oaks, CA: Sage.

Massumi, B. (2002). *A shock to thought: Expression after Deleuze and Guattari.* New York: Routledge.

Maxwell, J. A. (2004). *Qualitative research design: An interactive approach* (2nd ed.). Thousand Oaks, CA: Sage.

Mayan, M. J. (2009). *Essentials of qualitative inquiry.* Walnut Creek, CA: Left Coast Press.

McDonough, P. M. (1997). *Choosing colleges: How social class and schools structure opportunity.* Albany, NY: State University of New York Press.

McDonough, P. M., Antonio, A. L., and Walpole, M. (1998). College rankings: Democratized college knowledge for whom? *Research in Higher Education, 39*(5), 513–537.

McIntyre, A. (2008). *Participatory action research.* Thousand Oaks, CA: Sage.

McLaughlin, D., and Tierney, W. G. (Ed.). (1993). *Naming silenced lives: Personal narratives and the process of educational change.* New York: Routledge.

Merriam, S. B. (2002). *Qualitative research in practice: Examples for discussion and analysis.* San Francisco: Jossey-Bass.

Merriam, S. B. (2009). *Qualitative research: A guide to design and Implementation* (3rd ed.). San Francisco: Jossey-Bass.

Meyerson, D. E. (2008). *Rocking the boat: How to effect change without making trouble.* Boston: Harvard Business School Press.

Miles, M. B., and Huberman, A. M. (1994). *Qualitative data analysis: An expanded sourcebook* (2nd ed.). Thousand Oaks, CA: Sage.

Milner, H. R. (2007). Race, culture, and researcher positionality: Working through dangers seen, unseen, and unforeseen. *Educational Researcher, 36*(7), 388–400.

Morgan, K. J. (2004). The research assessment exercise in English universities, 2001. *Higher Education: The International Journal of Higher Education and Educational Planning, 48*(4), 461–482.

Morphew, C. C., and Eckel, P. D. (Eds.). (2009). *Privatizing the public university: Perspectives from across the academy.* Baltimore: Johns Hopkins University Press.

Morse, J. M., and others. (2009). *Developing grounded theory: The second generation.* Walnut Creek, CA: Left Coast Press.

Mosteller, F., and Boruch, R. (Eds.). (2002). *Evidence matters: Randomized trials in education research.* Washington, DC: Brookings Institution Press.

Moustakas, C. E. (1994). *Phenomenological research methods.* Thousand Oaks, CA: Sage.

National Research Council (NRC). (2002). *Scientific research in education.* Washington, DC: National Academy Press.

Nelson, C. (2004). The brave new world of research surveillance. *Qualitative Inquiry, 10*(2), 207–218.

No Child Left Behind Act of 2001, Pub. L. No. 107–110, 115 Stat. 1425 (2002).

Noblit, G. W., Flores, S. Y., and Murillo, E. G. (2004). *Postcritical ethnography: An introduction.* Cress, NJ: Hampton.

Nora, A. (2011). 2010–2011 Editorial Report. *Review of Higher Education.*

Norris, J. (2009). *Playbuilding as qualitative research: A participatory arts-based approach.* Walnut Creek, CA: Left Coast Press.

O'Connor, J. (2004). Success and challenges of community-based teaching, learning and research: A national perspective. In J. A. Galura, P. A. Pasque, D. Schoem, and J. Howard (Eds.), *Engaging the whole of service-learning, diversity, and learning communities* (pp. 14–19). Ann Arbor, MI: OCSL Press.

O'Connor, D. L., and O'Neill, B. J. (2004). Toward social justice—Teaching qualitative research. *Journal of Teaching in Social Work, 24*(3), 19–33.

Page, R. N. (2001). Reshaping graduate preparation in educational research methods: One school's experience. *Educational Researcher, 30*(5), 19–25.

Pallas, A. M. (2001). Preparing education doctoral students for epistemological diversity. *Educational Researcher, 30*(5), 6–11.

Pasque, P. A. (2010a). *American higher education, leadership, and policy: Critical issues and the public good.* New York: Palgrave Macmillan.

Pasque, P. A. (2010b). Collaborative approaches to community change. In H. E. Fitzgerald, C. Burack, and S. Siefer (Eds.), *Handbook of engaged scholarship: Contemporary landscapes, future directions: Vol. II. Community-campus partnerships* (pp. 295–310). East Lansing, MI: Michigan State University Press.

Pasque, P. A. (forthcoming). (Re)membering and (re)living: A methodological exploration of postmodern and constructivist feminist approaches to interviewing women leaders in higher education. *Journal About Women in Higher Education.*

Pasque, P. A., Carducci, R., Gildersleeve, R. E., and Kuntz, A. K. (2011). Disrupting the ethical imperatives of "junior" critical qualitative scholars in the era of conservative modernization. *Qualitative Inquiry, 17*(7), 571–588.

Pasque, P. A., Kuntz, A., Carducci, R., and Gildersleeve, R. E. (2008, November). Critical qualitative scholars connecting research and practice in the era of conservative modernization. Symposium presented at the Association for the Study of Higher Education, Jacksonville, FL.

Patton, M. Q. (2002). *Qualitative research and evaluation methods* (3rd ed.). Thousand Oaks, CA: Sage.

Pink, S. (2009). *Doing sensory ethnography*. Thousand Oaks, CA: Sage.

Pollio, H. R., Henley, T. B., and Thompson, C. J. (1997). *The phenomenology of everyday life*. Cambridge, MA: University Press.

Potts, K., and Brown, L. (2005). Becoming an anti-oppressive researcher. In L. Brown and S. Strega (Eds.), *Research as resistance: Critical, indigenous, and anti-oppressive approaches* (pp. 255–286). Toronto: Canadian Scholars' Press.

Powell, W. W., and Owen-Smith, J. (2002). The new world of knowledge production in the life sciences. In S. Britt (Ed.), *The future of the city of intellect: The changing American university* (pp. 107–130). Stanford, CA: Stanford University Press.

Reading Excellence Act of 1999, Pub. L. 105–277.

Reed-Danahay, D. E. (1997). *Auto/ethnography: Rewriting the self and the social*. New York: Berg.

Rhoads, R., and Torres, C. (Eds.). (2005). *The university, state, and market: The political economy of globalization in the Americas*. Stanford, CA: Stanford University Press.

Richardson, L., and St. Pierre, E. A. (2005). Writing: A method of inquiry. In N. K. Denzin and Y. S. Lincoln (Eds.), *The Sage handbook of qualitative inquiry* (3rd ed., pp. 959–978). Thousand Oaks, CA: Sage.

Rosenau, P. M. (1992). *Post-modernism and the social sciences: Insights, inroads, and intrusions*. Princeton, NJ: Princeton University Press.

Rossman, G., and Rallis, S. (2003). *Learning in the field: An introduction to qualitative research* (2nd ed.). Thousand Oaks, CA: Sage.

Rossman, G. B., and Rallis, S. F. (2011). *Learning in the field: An introduction to qualitative research* (3rd ed.). Thousand Oaks, CA: Sage.

Rowley, L. L. (2000). The relationship between universities and black urban communities: The class of two cultures. *Urban Review, 32*(1), 45–62.

Salzman, P. C. (2002). On reflexivity. *American Anthropologist, 104*(3), 805–813.

Schram, T. H. (2006). *Conceptualizing and proposing qualitative research* (2nd ed.). Upper Saddle River, NJ: Pearson Prentice Hall.

Schrecker, E. (2001). From the editor: Selling out? *Academe, 87*(5), 2.

Schwandt, T. (2006). Opposition redirected. *International Journal of Qualitative Studies in Education, 19*(6), 803–810.

Schwandt, T. (1999). On understanding understanding. *Qualitative Inquiry, 5*(4), 451–464.

Schwandt, T. A. (2007). *The Sage dictionary of qualitative inquiry* (3rd ed.). Thousand Oaks, CA: Sage.

Slavin, R. (2002). Evidence-based educational policies: Transforming educational practice and research. *Educational Researcher, 31*(7), 15–21.

Slaughter, S. (2001). Professional values and the allure of the market [Electronic version]. *Academe, 87*(5), 22–26.

Slaughter, S., and Leslie, L. L. (1997). *Academic capitalism: Politics, policies, and the entrepreneurial university*. Baltimore: Johns Hopkins University Press.

Slaughter S., and Rhoades, G. (2004). *Academic capitalism and the new economy: Markets, state and higher education.* Baltimore: Johns Hopkins University Press.

Smith, L. T. (1999). Decolonizing methodologies: Research and indigenous people. New York: Zed.

Soja, E. (1989). *Postmodern geographies: The reassertion of space in critical social theory.* New York: Verso.

Soja, E. (1996). *Thirdspace: Journeys to Los Angeles and other real-and-imagined places.* Oxford, UK: Blackwell.

Soja, E. (2000). *Postmetropolis: Critical studies of cities and regions.* Oxford, UK: Blackwell.

Solórzano, D., and Delgado Bernal, D. (2001). Critical race theory, transformational resistance and social justice: Chicana and Chicano students in an urban context. *Urban Education, 36,* 308–342.

Solórzano, D., and Yosso, T. (2001). Critical race and LatCrit theory and method: Counter-storytelling Chicana and Chicano graduate school experiences. *International Journal of Qualitative Studies in Education, 14*(4), 471–495.

Solórzano, D., and Yosso, T. (2002). A critical race counterstory of affirmative action in higher education. *Equity and Excellence in Education, 35*(2), 155–168.

Somerville, M. (2007). Postmodern emergence. *International Journal of Qualitative Studies in Education, 20*(2), 225–243.

Spry, T. (2011). *Body, paper, stage: Writing and performing autoethnography.* Walnut Creek, CA: Left Coast Press.

St. Pierre, E. (1997). Circling the text: Nomadic writing practices. *Qualitative Inquiry, 3*(4), 403–418.

St. Pierre, E. A. (2004). Refusing alternatives: A science of contestation. *Qualitative Inquiry, 10*(1), 130–139.

Stage, F. K. (2007). Editor's notes. In F. K. Stage (Ed.). *New Directions for Institutional Research,* No. 133 (pp. 1–3). San Francisco: Jossey-Bass.

Stake, R. E. (1995). *The art of case study research.* Thousand Oaks, CA: Sage.

Stake, R. E. (2008). Qualitative cases studies. In N. K. Denzin and Y. S. Lincoln (Eds.), *Strategies of qualitative inquiry* (3rd ed., pp. 119–150). Thousand Oaks, CA: Sage.

Stanley, C. A. (2007). When counter narratives meet master narratives in the journal editorial-review process. *Educational Researcher, 36*(1), 14–24.

Stein, D. G. (Ed.). (2004). *Buying in or selling out? The commercialization of the American research university.* New Brunswick, NJ: Rutgers University Press.

Stewart, D. L. (2008). Being all of me: Black students negotiating multiple identities. *Journal of Higher Education, 79*(2), 183–207.

Strega, S. (2005). The view from the poststructural margins: Epistemology and methodology reconsidered. In L. Brown and S. Strega (Eds.), *Research as resistance: Critical, indigenous, and anti-oppressive approaches* (pp. 199–235). Toronto: Canadian Scholars' Press.

Talburt, S. (2000). *Subject to Identity: Knowledge, sexuality, and academic practices in higher education.* Albany, NY: SUNY Press.

Talburt, S. (2004). Ethnographic responsibility without the "real." *Journal of Higher Education, 75*(1), 80–103.

Teddlie, C., and Tashakkori, A. (2011). Mixed methods research: Contemporary issues in an emerging field. In N. K. Denzin and Y. S. Lincoln (Eds.), *The Sage handbook of qualitative research* (4th ed., pp. 285–299). Thousand Oaks, CA: Sage.

Temple, P. (2008). Learning spaces in higher education: An under-researched topic. *London Review of Education, 6*(3), 229–241.

Temple, P. (2009). From space to place: University performance and its built environment. *Higher Education Policy, 22*(2), 209–223.

Thomas, G., and James, D. (2006). Reinventing grounded theory: Some questions about theory, ground and discovery. *British Educational Research Journal, 32*(6), 767–795.

Tierney, W. G. (2006). The examined university: Process and change in higher education. In W. G. Tierney (Ed.), *Governance and the public good* (pp. 1–10). Albany, NY: State University of New York Press.

Tierney, W. G., and Corwin, Z. B. (2007). The tension between academic freedom and institutional review boards. *Qualitative Inquiry, 13*(3), 388–398.

Torrance, H. (2008). Building confidence in qualitative research: Engaging the demands of policy. *Qualitative Inquiry, 14*(4), 507–527.

Torrance, H. (2011). Qualitative research, science, and government: Evidence, criteria, policy, and politics. In N. K. Denzin and Y. S. Lincoln. (Eds.), *The Sage handbook of qualitative research* (4th ed., pp. 569–580). Thousand Oaks, CA: Sage.

Valenzuela, A. (1999). *Subtractive schooling: U.S.–Mexican youth and the politics of caring.* Albany, NY: State University of New York Press.

Van Maanen, J. (2011). *Tales of the field: On writing ethnography* (2nd ed.). Chicago: University of Chicago Press.

van Manen, M. (1990). Researching lived experience: Human science for an action sensitive pedagogy. Albany, NY: State University of New York Press.

van Manen, M. (2002). *Writing in the dark: Phenomenological studies in interpretive inquiry.* London, ON: Althouse.

van Manen, M. (2007). Phenomenology of practice. *Phenomenology and Practice, 1*(1), 11–30.

Wagner, R (2011). Is your profundity a trammel or a treasure? Lessons in ability and identity. In P. A. Pasque and M. Errington Nicholson (Eds.), *Empowering women in higher education and student affairs: Theory, research, narratives and practice from feminist perspectives* (pp. 250–251). Sterling, VA: Stylus/American College Personnel Association.

Waitere, H. J., and others. (2011). Choosing whether to resist or reinforce the new managerialism: The impact of performance-based research funding on academic identity. *Higher Education Research and Development, 30*(2), 205–217.

Walker, A., and Zinn, H. (2010/1996). A conversation with [Alice Walker and] Howard Zinn at city arts and lectures. In R. P. Byrd (Ed.), *The world has changed: Conversations with Alice Walker* (pp. 146–158). New York: New Press.

Warren, C.A.B., and Karner, T. X. (2010). *Discovering qualitative methods: Field research, interviews and analysis* (2nd ed.). New York: Oxford University Press.

Washburn, J. (2005). *University, Inc.* New York: Basic Books.

Weiss, R. S. (1994). Learning from strangers: The art and method of qualitative interview studies. New York: Free Press.

Wetherell, M., Taylor, S., and Yates, S. J. (Eds.). (2001). *Discourse as data: A guide for analysis.* Thousand Oaks, CA: Sage.

Wiles, R., Pain, H., and Crow, G. (2010). *Innovation in qualitative research methods: A narrative review.* Southampton, UK: ESRC National Centre for Research Methods.

Wilson, S. (2009). *Research is ceremony: Indigenous research methods.* Halifax, NS, Canada: Fernwood.

Wilson, W. A., and Yellow Bird, M. (2005*). For indigenous eyes only: A decolonization handbook.* Sante Fe, NM: School of American Research Press.

Winkle-Wagner, R. (2009). The perpetual homelessness of college experiences: Tensions between home and campus for African American women. *Review of Higher Education, 33*(1), 1–36.

Wong, A. S. (2011). In flux: Racial identity construction among Chinese American and Filipina/o American undergraduates. (Unpublished doctoral dissertation). University of Michigan, Ann Arbor.

Wright, H. K. (2003). An endarkened feminist epistemology? Identity, difference and the politics of representation in educational research. *Qualitative Studies in Education, 16*(2), 197–214.

Yakaboski, T. (2011). "Quietly stripping the pastels": The undergraduate gender gap. *Review of Higher Education, 34*(4), 555–580.

Yin, R. K. (2003). *Case study research: Design and methods.* (3rd ed.). Thousand Oaks, CA: Sage.

Yin, R. K. (2009). *Case study research: Design and methods* (4th ed.). Thousand Oaks, CA: Sage.

Young, I. M. (1990). *Justice and the politics of difference.* Princeton, NJ: Princeton University Press.

Young, I. M. (2010). Five faces of oppression. In M. Adams, W. J. Blumenfeld, C. Castaneda, H W. Hackman, M. L. Peters, and X. Zuniga (Eds.), *Readings for diversity and social justice: An anthology on racism, anti-Semitism, sexism, heterosexism, ableism, and classism* (pp. 35–45). New York: Routledge.

Zemsky, R. M. (2005). The dog that doesn't bark: Why markets neither limit prices nor promote educational quality. In J. C. Burke (Ed.), *Achieving accountability in higher education: Balancing public, academic, and market demands* (pp. 275–295). San Francisco: Jossey-Bass.

Name Index

A

Abes, E., 64
Alemán, E. Jr., 70
Althusser, L., 45
Antonio, A. L., 9
Anyon, J., 28
Apple, M. W., 1, 8, 10, 48, 50, 51, 56, 58, 62, 63, 64, 76, 85–86
Arminio, J., 23–25, 47, 76
Armsby, P., 76
Atkinson, P., 4
Ayers, D. F., 58

B

Barad, K., 28, 44
Bartik, T. J., 58
Battiste, M., 28
Bennoff, R. J., 59
Best, S., 26
Bijian, Z., 9
Biklen, S. K., 5
Blake, E. C., 42
Bloch, M., 49, 50, 53, 65, 71
Bloom, L. R., 7, 12
Bogdan, R., 5
Bok, D., 9, 48, 57
Boruch, R., 50
Bowers, B., 5
Brandl, J., 58, 59
Brayboy, B. M. J., 64

Brinkmann, S., 44
Broadhead, L., 52
Brodeur, C. W., 67, 68, 69, 79, 80, 86
Broido, E., 26
Brown, C., 9
Brown, L., 11, 28, 50
Brown, S., 52
Brydon-Miller, M., 28, 67
Burbules, N. C., 8
Burke, J. C., 1
Butler, C., 26

C

Cameron, D., 5
Cannella, G. S., 6, 8, 10, 13, 28, 47, 48, 50, 51, 52, 53, 56, 59, 65, 66, 78, 79, 80, 81, 84, 86, 87
Carducci, R., 4
Carducci, R., 4, 10
Carroll Klassan, A., 59, 61
Charmaz, K., 5, 30
Chase, S. E., 4
Chaudhry, L. N., 76
Cheek, J., 1, 48, 51, 52, 57, 58, 60, 69, 71, 78, 84, 85
Chesler, M., 80
Chomsky, N., 31
Clarke, A. E., 5
Clegg Smith, K., 59, 61
Clough, P. T., 5, 11

J

Jackson, A. Y., 39, 40, 64
Jackson, B., 26
James, D., 30, 31
Johnson, R. B., 59
Johnson, T. S., 64
Johnstone, B., 5
Jones, S. R., 23–25, 47, 76

K

Karner, T. X., 5
Kasch, D., 64
Kellner, D., 26
Kezar, A., 80, 84
Kezar, A. J., 81
Kincheloe, J., 7
Kincheloe, J. L., 27, 50, 54
Kirp, D. L., 57
Kmiec, C., 67, 68, 69, 79, 80, 86
Koro-Ljungberg, M., 67, 68, 69, 79, 80, 81, 86
Kouritzin, S. G., 89
Krugman, P., 8
Kuntz, A., 4, 35, 37, 41, 42
Kuntz, A. K., 4
Kuntz, A. M., 10

L

Lather, P., 10, 27, 40, 50, 76, 81
Leslie, L. L., 9, 48, 58
Lester, J., 80, 84
Levin, J. S., 57
Levin, M., 59, 69, 71, 86, 87
Lewis, A., 80
Lightfoot, C., 4, 5
Lincoln, Y., 3, 6, 23, 24, 25, 47
Lincoln, Y. S., 6, 8, 10, 13, 19, 25, 47, 48, 50, 51, 52, 53, 56, 59, 60, 64, 65, 66, 68, 78, 79, 80, 81, 84, 86, 87, 91
Lofland, J., 4
Lofland, L., 4
Lovell, C. D., 19, 20, 30
Luu, D. T., 57, 58

M

Madison, D. S., 28, 86
Mahbubani, K., 9
Manning, K., 26
Marcus, G. E., 32
Marshall, C., 5, 23, 47
Marshall, J., 5
Massey, D., 41, 42
Massumi, B., 39
Maxwell, J. A., 47
Mayan, M. J., 24
Mazzei, L. A., 39, 40, 64
McDonough, P. M., 9
McIntyre, A., 28
McLaren, P., 27, 50, 54
McLaughlin, D., 64
Merriam, S. B., 4, 47
Meyerson, D. E., 84
Miles, M. B., 5
Milner, H. R., 76
Morgan, K. J., 1, 51, 52
Morphew, C. C., 57
Morse, J. M., 5
Mosteller, F., 50
Moustakas, C. E., 4, 26
Murillo, E. G., 11
Museus, S. D., 59
Myers, W. B., 86

N

Nelson, C., 67
Noblit, G. W., 11
Nora, A., 19
Norman, R., 89
Norris, J., 5, 28

O

O'Connor, D. L., 81
O'Connor, J., 21
O'Neill, B. J., 81
Onwuegbuzie, A. J., 59
Owen-Smith, J., 58

Subject Index

A

Academic capitalism, 5, 8, 9, 45, 56–66, 69, 71–78, 83, 88, 91; cloaking of, within commonsense rhetoric, 62–63; and critical qualitative higher education scholars, 65–73; escalating influence of, 56, 61–62, 65; methodological implications of, 56–61; and neoliberal principles, 57–58; and reflexivity, 78–79; rise of, 48–49; use of term, 56–57

Academic freedom: constraints imposed by IRB processes, 68; and methodological conservatism, 66; norm of, regarding critical qualitative researchers, 70–71; scholarly punishments, 65

Academic publishing process, 69–70

Agency, 12, 17, 62, 77

American Civil Rights Institute, 62–63

American Education Research Association (AERA), 48, 52, 54–56

Arts-based inquiry, 28

Association for the Study of Higher Education (ASHE), 48

Australian Research Quality Framework, 52

Autoethnography, 28

Axiology, 21–22, 26, 76; and researcher's paradigms, 24

B

Banishment of critical scholars to disciplinary margins, 71–72

Best Practices for Mixed Methods Research in the Health Sciences (NIH), 61

Binary thinking, 21

Breaking Bread: Insurgent Black Intellectual Life (hooks/West), 35

C

Campus approval process, for engaging in human subjects research, 66

Cartesian Duality, 22, 34, 44; and innovation, 36–38

China, and globalization, 9

Common Rule, 66–68; defined, 66

Communication skills, expansion of, 87

Conservative forces, and control over the academic endeavor, 1

Conservative modernization of education, 8, 10

Constructivism, 19, 25

Contemporary contexts of higher education research, and equity, 8

Content of research, and higher education scholars, 1–2

Counter-storytelling, 28

Critical education scholars, and expansion of communication skills, 87

Critical ethnography, 28

Critical higher education scholars: academic publishing process, 69–70; choice between methodological research and scientifically based educational research, 68; and cultivation of political

114

competencies, 84; defense of assumptions guiding their scholarship, 84; funded research, 68–69; and methodological conservatism, 65–73; and politics of knowledge, 84; pressure to adopt language/practices incongruent with methodological perspectives, 67–68

Critical inquiry, 25

Critical Lede, 86

Critical methodological training, expanded communication skills, 87

Critical qualitative higher education research, in era of methodological conservatism, 49–61

Critical qualitative higher education scholars: fostering change beyond campus, 80; and methodological conservatism, 65–73

Critical qualitative inquiry, 3–5, 13; changing responsibilities/emphases of higher education, 5; and construction of a unified voice, 39–40; and daily practices of intervention, 89; defined, 27; dialogue as an epistemological innovation, 34–35; epistemology, 32–34; for equity in higher education, 4; in an era of methodological conservatism, 49–61; promise/hope of, 27–29

Critical quantitative inquiry, 20–21; as nondeterministic process, 23; as response to traditional research paradigms, 13

Critical quantitative research, 5

Critical race theory, 25

Critical scholar's work, and critical inquiry, 66

Critical social science, defined, 66

Critical theory, 19, 25

Critical thought, and problematization, 5

Cultural studies, silencing of underreprese nt4ed groups, 27

Cycle of liberation (Harro), 77–79

Cycle of socialization (Harro), 27, 77–79

D

Dangers, 11–12, 36; embedded within the scientifically based educational research movement, 52; responding to, 12–13

Data collection, 23

Definition of Scientifically Based Research (AERA), 52–53

Dialogue: between constituencies, 85–86; and critical inquiry, 85–86; as epistemological innovation, 34–35; as insurrection, 34–35; political/ideological nature of, 13; reflective, 85

Disciplinary affiliation, and scholars challenging epistemological and methodological foundations, 73

Disciplinary margins: banishment of critical scholars to, 71–72; and contemporary dialogues, 55

Disciplining discourse regimes, of academic capitalism, 49–56, 83–84

Disinterestedness vs. critical engagement, 2

Doctoral coursework, and cultivation of political competencies, 85

Doctoral level research training, 84

Dominant inquiry, failure of, 20

E

Education Sciences Reform Act of 2002, 51

Educational policymaking, in U.S., 51

Educational research articles: and dominant knowledge regimes, 69; on graduate preparation in educational research methods, 82–83

Embodied innovation, 43–45

Epistemology, 21–22, 26, 76, 82; and critical qualitative work, 32–34; and researcher's paradigms, 24

Equity, 2–3, 6–10, 12; concerns, 7; and contemporary contexts of higher education research, 8; defined, 2; and methodology, 31; and organization/governance of higher-education institutions, 7; resistance to definition, 7; and social justice/social change, 7–8

Ethnography, 25; auto-, 28; critical, 28; performance, 28
Existential phenomenology, 25
Expansion: of academic capitalism, 59; of communication skills, 87
External funding, 68–69

F

Facebook, 86
Faculty methodological conversations, 82
Favoritism, displayed by funding agencies, 61
Feminism, 24; articles including language of, 20; discourse, 25; silencing of underrepresented groups, 27
fullparticipation.net, 86
Funding, 1, 68–69; and disenfranchising of collaborative work, 17; and equity, 7; external, 68–69; favoritism toward mixed methods research, 61; and neoliberal agenda of market supremacy, scholars contesting, 59; pressure, to foster a shift in faculty identities, 69; private enterprise's interest in, 1; protocols, 61; and research agendas, 78–79; of science-based educational research, federal preference for, 51

G

Getting Lost: Feminist Efforts Towards a Double(d) Science (Lather), 40
Global audit culture, 51–52; in U.S., 52
Global knowledge economy, 56
Globalization, 3, 8–9, *See also* Academic capitalism; and academic capitalism, 9; and China, 9; of higher education, 8–9; influence on American higher education, 9
Grounded theory, 30–31; and constructivist approach, 30; and growth of qualitative inquiry, 31

H

Hermeneutic phenomenology, 25
Hidden research agenda, 26–27
Higher education: as

applied/interdisciplinary field of study, 17–18; qualitative inquiry for equity in, 1–15; social science methods of study of, 17–18
Historically marginalized communities, and methodological conservatism, 61–65
Human subjects, research, campus approval process for engaging in, 66
Humanist subjects, 38–39; defined, 38
Humanities Standards, *See Standards for Reporting on Humanities-Oriented Research in AERA Publications* (AERA)
Hyperpessimistic activism, 11–12, 73

I

In/equity in higher education, 2–5, 10, 14, 18, 27, 50, 88–89; addressing via research processes and products, 57, 59, 65, 72; and methodological conservativism, 73, 75
Indigenous methodologies, 28
Inequitable status quo, maintained by economic/political elite, 71
Injustice, and American higher education, 12
Innovation, 31; and Cartesian Duality, 36–38; defined, 29; dialogue as an epistemological innovation, 34–35; embodied, 43–45; and epistemology, 32–34; methodological, 31; poststructural voices, 38–41; revolutionary subjects, 35–38; spatial, 41–43
Innovative research, 29–45
Inquiry as political activity, 2
Inquiry practice, 2
Institute of Education Sciences (U.S. Dept. of Education), 51
Institutional intervention, 79–81
Institutional review board (IRB) processes, 67–72; and critical higher education scholars, 67–68; disciplining function of, 67; participating in process, 79–80
Interactive triad, 13–14, 21
International Monetary Fund, 9
Interpretivism, use of term, 25

About the Authors

Penny A. Pasque is an assistant professor in Educational Leadership and Policy Studies and Women's and Gender Studies/Center for Social Justice at the University of Oklahoma. Her research addresses in/equities in higher education, dis/connections between higher education and society, and complexities in critical qualitative inquiry. Her latest book is *American Higher Education, Leadership, and Policy: Critical Issues and the Public Good* (Palgrave Macmillan).

Rozana Carducci is an assistant professor in Educational Leadership and Policy Analysis at the University of Missouri. Her research interests include higher education leadership, academic capitalism, and the politics of inquiry.

Aaron M. Kuntz is an assistant professor in Educational Studies at the University of Alabama. His research interests include critical geography, academic citizenship and activism, materialist methodologies, and critical inquiry.

Ryan Evely Gildersleeve strives to be a social scient<art>ist while playing the role of associate professor and director of the Center for K–16 Education Policy and Research at the University of Texas at Arlington. His research focuses on educational opportunity and critical inquiry. He is the author of *Fracturing Opportunity: Mexican Migrant Students and College-going Literacy* (Peter Lang Publishers). He is a graduate of Occidental College.

These authors are part of a collaborative research collective known as the Disruptive Dialogue Project. All authors contributed equally to this manuscript, but have elected an egalitarian authorship rotation order among and across different publication products.

About the ASHE Higher Education Report Series

Since 1983, the ASHE (formerly ASHE-ERIC) Higher Education Report Series has been providing researchers, scholars, and practitioners with timely and substantive information on the critical issues facing higher education. Each monograph presents a definitive analysis of a higher education problem or issue, based on a thorough synthesis of significant literature and institutional experiences. Topics range from planning to diversity and multiculturalism, to performance indicators, to curricular innovations. The mission of the Series is to link the best of higher education research and practice to inform decision making and policy. The reports connect conventional wisdom with research and are designed to help busy individuals keep up with the higher education literature. Authors are scholars and practitioners in the academic community. Each report includes an executive summary, review of the pertinent literature, descriptions of effective educational practices, and a summary of key issues to keep in mind to improve educational policies and practice.

The Series is one of the most peer reviewed in higher education. A National Advisory Board made up of ASHE members reviews proposals. A National Review Board of ASHE scholars and practitioners reviews completed manuscripts. Six monographs are published each year and they are approximately 144 pages in length. The reports are widely disseminated through Jossey-Bass and John Wiley & Sons, and they are available online to subscribing institutions through Wiley Online Library (http://wileyonlinelibrary.com).

Call for Proposals

The ASHE Higher Education Report Series is actively looking for proposals. We encourage you to contact one of the editors, Dr. Kelly Ward (kaward@wsu.edu) or Dr. Lisa Wolf-Wendel (lwolf@ku.edu), with your ideas.

Recent Titles

ASHE HIGHER EDUCATION REPORT

ORDER FORM SUBSCRIPTION AND SINGLE ISSUES

DISCOUNTED BACK ISSUES:

Use this form to receive 20% off all back issues of *ASHE Higher Education Report*.
All single issues priced at **$23.20** (normally $29.00)

TITLE	ISSUE NO.	ISBN

Call 888-378-2537 or see mailing instructions below. When calling, mention the promotional code JBNND to receive your discount. For a complete list of issues, please visit www.josseybass.com/go/aehe

SUBSCRIPTIONS: (1 YEAR, 6 ISSUES)

☐ New Order   ☐ Renewal

U.S.	☐ Individual: $174	☐ Institutional: $281
CANADA/MEXICO	☐ Individual: $174	☐ Institutional: $341
ALL OTHERS	☐ Individual: $210	☐ Institutional: $392

Call 888-378-2537 or see mailing and pricing instructions below.
Online subscriptions are available at www.onlinelibrary.wiley.com

ORDER TOTALS:

Issue / Subscription Amount: $ _____

Shipping Amount: $ _____
(for single issues only – subscription prices include shipping)

Total Amount: $ _____

SHIPPING CHARGES:	
First Item	$6.00
Each Add'l Item	$2.00

(No sales tax for U.S. subscriptions. Canadian residents, add GST for subscription orders. Individual rate subscriptions must be paid by personal check or credit card. Individual rate subscriptions may not be resold as library copies.)

BILLING & SHIPPING INFORMATION:

☐ **PAYMENT ENCLOSED:** *(U.S. check or money order only. All payments must be in U.S. dollars.)*

☐ **CREDIT CARD:**   ☐ VISA   ☐ MC   ☐ AMEX

Card number _____ Exp. Date _____

Card Holder Name _____ Card Issue # _____

Signature _____ Day Phone _____

☐ **BILL ME:** *(U.S. institutional orders only. Purchase order required.)*

Purchase order # _____
    Federal Tax ID 13559302 • GST 89102-8052

Name _____

Address _____

Phone _____   E-mail _____

Copy or detach page and send to: **John Wiley & Sons, One Montgomery Street, Suite 1200, San Francisco, CA 94104-4594**

Order Form can also be faxed to: **888-481-2665**

PROMO JBNND

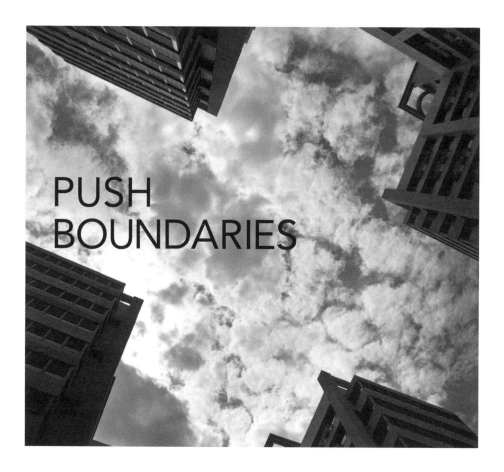